DETAIL research
Building the Future

The Future of Building: Perspectives

Methods, Objectives, Prospects

The advent
of a new
period only
occurs after
long and
quiet prepara-
tory work.

Le Corbusier

Introduction

Sandra Hofmeister

Architecture is a future-oriented discipline. It sets the course of development of cities, buildings, and spaces that shape the world of tomorrow, influencing them in a positive or negative way. The foundations of built spaces and future living environments are laid in the here and now. Architects and clients, the building industry, and researchers face a number of challenges: to be progressive in their reaction to developments and requirements, to provide strategies for dealing with these, and to find intelligent ways of responding to social, ecological, and economic trends and requirements.

Being a future-oriented discipline, the core motivation behind architecture is idealistic in nature. It is concerned with an improvement – of whatever kind – of the present condition and seeks progress. The definition of this progress is dependent on era and region, state of knowledge and client, as well as being based on previously specified tasks and options. What the world of tomorrow will look like, what the objectives and living environments created by its spaces, its urban and spatial structures will be, as well as the means and resources required for their construction – all this is part of a social discourse and decision-making process. This, in turn, continuously sets new priorities and calls for re-alignment, revision, and adaptation with regard to specific aims and methods. The future of architecture is not a static category, but instead a negotiable variable, and therefore a process that begins in the present.

What are the particular future positions that we specify today, which objectives do we define, and with which methods and resources do we aim to realise them? What exactly are the social requirements and challenges faced by all those involved – be it during construction, planning, design, or in the building industry? Which technologies, materials, and possibilities come into question? Which scientific methods can be used to forecast future developments, to predict trends, and how do we react to these?

All these questions were discussed by experts during a six-day symposium entitled 'Future Research in Architecture' held in January 2011. The presentations, discussions, and debates hosted by DETAIL during the BAU Trade Fair envisioned the future as category from various perspectives – not in the sense of a utopia or a vague sketch, but based on precise findings, as well as experiences and research results. Architects and specialist planners, product designers, and researchers from various institutions and companies presented their views on the future of building in talks and discussions. This event resulted in a multi-faceted image of the architecture of tomorrow, in the course of which individual aspects were elucidated, discussions were engaged in, experiences were shared, and needs and approaches were formulated. In fact, the symposium was the actual point of origin for the interdisciplinary platform 'DETAIL research. Building the Future'. This platform aims to bundle future-relevant topics and reports from the world of practice and research. The focus is on exchange as well as transfer of knowledge. This collaboration was transferred to the virtual realm as an Online Forum created specifically for the above described purposes. In cooperation with experts and decision makers in research, practice, and industry as partners, the forum serves as an information platform for gaining insight into future-relevant studies and practical approaches.

News, innovative examples, and research results are collected at www.detailresearch.de and presented as a publicly accessible network including a research archive.

This publication is a further building block intended to extend and strengthen the discourse on the future of building. Various positions are gathered with the intention of linking them, discovering synergies and complementary issues, presenting results, and raising further questions. For this purpose, the contributions to discussions and lectures at the symposium have been expanded by various topics and perspectives, creating a multi-faceted panorama of the future of building. While this collection doesn't intend to cover every aspect, it nevertheless hopes to provoke thought in specific areas as well as offer related outlook. In addition to studies by a number of institutions in higher education and research, this book also presents practical experiences of architects and specialist planners, general considerations regarding social perspectives, and scientific methodology for forecasting trends. Various approaches from the industry, differing in scale, are also taken into account. As drivers of innovation, these are important participants in precisely defining and manifesting the living spaces of the future.

The individual contributions deal with the methods and objectives of the future of building and the design of living environments. They consider different views and perspectives relating to partially complementary fields, links between which are identified by means of colour-coded text. The programming aspects of planning, building, and production processes are considered against the background of several research findings and reports from practice. They also take into account the interaction of programming and material, as well as the possibilities of automated production and parametric design systems. Individualisation trends are identified and discussed with regard to their future potential, either as competition factors or in terms of the freedom in adopting a subjective design perspective. Planning priorities that are oriented on societal and economic aspects supplement the discussion with political targets. These, in return, are related to future building tasks and are considered relevant with regard to growth and shrinkage scenarios, as well as energy and local resources issues. The scientific topic of trend research, which projects a precise image of the future using scenario techniques and monitoring, complements the micro-perspective of individual contributions and studies presented in this book. As result, a meta-discussion is included that remains open for future discussion. If the future of building starts in the present, then the 'Positions on the Future of Building' aim to illustrate snapshots of the present while examining their potential for the future.

In the first issue of 'L'Esprit Nouveau' in 1920, Le Corbusier proclaimed: "A great era has just begun. There exists a new spirit." A good 90 years later, this categorical statement is still relevant for many aspects of architecture and building, although the conditions and parameters certainly have changed. In an age of digital programming, globalisation, and demographic change, the tasks, methods, and sometimes even the aims of building and planning have shifted. Numerous processes and procedures in planning, production, and building now merge and thereby create the conditions and foundations of a future, the possibilities and requirements of which are already clearly evident in many ways today.

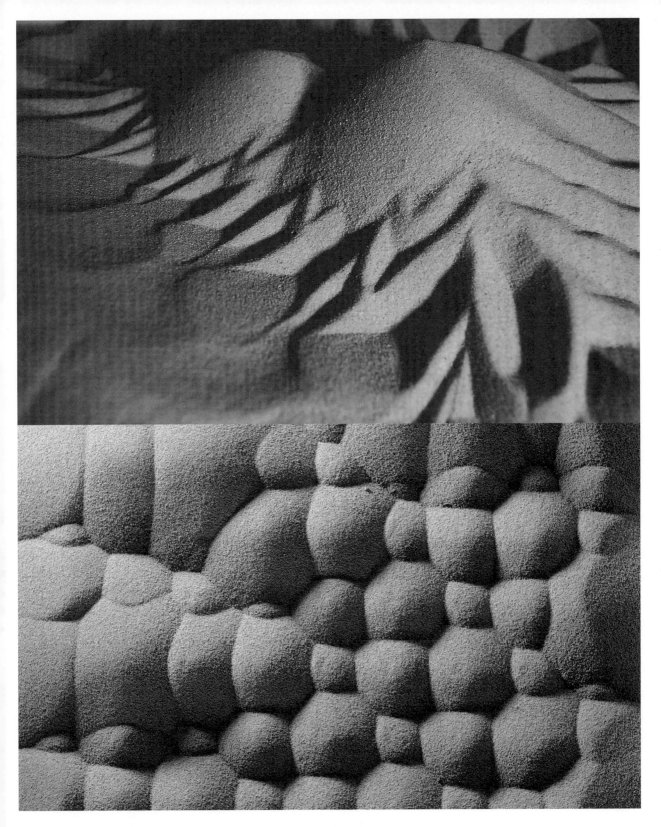

'Procedural landscapes'   **6|1** Cast concrete prototype module on an architectural scale
7|1 Detail of a sandscape   **7|2** Geometrically controlled precision of a digitally fabricated sandscape

Operationality of Data and Material in the Digital Age

Text Matthias Kohler, Fabio Gramazio, Jan Willmann

1

The combination of the terms 'digital' and 'materiality' used here originates in a publication by Fabio Gramazio and Matthias Kohler, 'Digital Materiality in Architecture' (Baden 2007). Combining these previously separate terms aims at achieving a specific meaning for architecture in the age of its digital fabrication capacity, beyond an update of familiar rhetoric in abidance to old functions and contents. Digital materiality consequently only gains its autonomous characteristic by being embedded in its antinomies. This means, with reference to architecture, that extended forms of interpretation can be derived and systematic differentiations, as opposed to generalisation of purely digital or materialistic aspects, for instance, can be made.

The synthesis of data and material is perhaps something that the early digital age failed to achieve. Yet now, architecture provocatively, playfully, and even sensuously fulfils this promise. With 'architectural computation', 'mass customisation', and 'digital fabrication' the issue of materiality in the information age has been revived. The issue of concern here is 'digital materiality'.[1] This describes a changed role of material processes in architecture. Digital materiality can be observed in all sorts of media-related, spatial, or structural forms. The fact remains that in the digital age the increasing influence of digital materiality on architecture implies that the interpretation of data and materials is extended from being merely supplementary to an inherent, and therefore significant expression of architecture. Digital materiality advances from solely being a rhetorical figure in the digital discourse to actually representing a value in itself. The moment that the two apparently separate worlds meet during the interplay of digital and material processes associated with design and building, digital materiality manifests. The aim is to enrich material with information, to 'inform' material, so to speak, and thereby define the process of development of architectural structure. This synthesis is not bound to a function assigned a priori, but occurs as process through the linkage of data and material, of programming and construction.

Therefore, the synthesis of data and material appears in a new light, as a reciprocal structuring of architecture and its material forms of manifestation.[2] Viewed in this context, digital materiality should not only be regarded as a virtual construct, but as set of procedures requiring specific design processes and constructive correlations. Thus, it isn't accidental or supplemental, or simply a process of beautification. Instead, it corresponds to an interaction of legitimate processes and material properties that can be analysed and realised on an architectural scale. This is also the basis for research carried out at the Professorship Gramazio & Kohler, Architecture and Digital Fabrication at the ETH Zurich. A central question is to what extent the difference between data and material can still be maintained. Digital materiality appears to rescind the often discussed comparison of programming and construction, of data and material, and instead open up new possibilities disclosed by current research in digital materiality, which depict new forms of a future constructional reality.

Transpositional potentials and additive structurings

When constructive principles are embedded, digital materiality receives more than only a supplemental or implementational function and gains its constructive status through the interaction of programming and material. As result, conceptual similarities between the manufacture of a building component and the programming of a computer can be identified. Similar to a computer programme executing different operations in a logical sequence, constructive principles can be specified that define the manufacture of architectural building components as consecutive manufacturing steps. The central aspect here is an additive principle that allows targeted control and manipulation of assembling complex architectural structures based on individual elements. This enables the creation of new spatial and functional configurations. Rather than the design of a shape, this relates to the design of a manufacturing process, which significantly informs the constructive organisation of a component and, to a similar extent, its execution. While defining significant parameters and dependencies, the architectural creative will remains characterised by precision and clarity. However, it is detached from formal specifications and transferred to a different (constructive) level. It becomes clear that questions on correlating data and material also have an inherent constructive meaning: this becomes apparent as a structuring liberated from formal specifications, i.e. as a result of a "demystified understanding of digital technologies and a liberated, autonomous utilisation of computers".[3]

2

This discussion is intended to provide clear proof that the synthesis of data and material is not a virtual accomplishment, but rather a 'material' one, i.e. real results are created. This was already conceptualised by Henri van de Velde at the beginning of the 20th century, who elevated production and material to an object of contemporary architecture and who saw an increasing supremacy in the position of engineers in the new production conditions of industrialisation. From this he concluded that the resulting limitation of architecture can only be solved in connection with constructive and functional technologies, in which the artist now appears as 'master builder' and the 'material' first has to be dematerialised for the sake of form, material, and construction, in order to revive it again at a later point in time, thereby adapting architecture to the new circumstances of the time. Cf.: van de Velde, Henri: 'Die Renaissance im modernen Kunstgewerbe.' [Renaissance in Modern Arts and Crafts.] Berlin 1901

For further aspects of the interconnection of planning, building, and fabrication processes cf. Industrialisation versus Individualisation » *p. 21, 25, Material, Information, Technology* » *p. 31, Parametric Design Systems* » *p. 43, Building Processes of Tomorrow* » *p. 126*

3

Gramazio, Fabio; Kohler, Matthias:
'Die Digitale Materialität der
Architektur.' [Digital Materiality in
Architecture.]
In: Arch+ 198–199/2010, p. 42f.

4

Semper, Gottfried: 'Der Stil in den
technischen und tektonischen
Künsten oder praktische Ästhetik'
[Style in Technical and Tectonic
Arts or Practical Aesthetics],
Volume 1. Munich 1878

5

The project 'The Sequential Structure' was developed as part of
a course at the ETH Zurich in 2010
(project manager: Michael Knauss;
students: Jonas Epper, Sofia Georga-
kopoulou, Benz Hubler, Jessica
Knobloch, Matthew Huber, Teresa
McWalters, Maria Vrontissi). Based
on physical hanging chain models
and their digital simulation, a temporary, walk-in wooden installation
for shading a sun-exposed terrace
was designed and built on a real
scale in collaboration with the
BLOCK Research Group at the ETH
Zurich. The structure consists of
individually stacked slats. As a shell
construction additively assembled
by an industrial robot, the structure
not only permits a structurally optimised multi-directional load transfer,
but also offers completely new
degrees of freedom of design using
the traditional resource timber.

6

The term 'implicitness' is intended
to imply two things: on the one hand,
the mimetic adaptation to current
technological and cultural relations
facilitated by the synthesis of data
and material, resulting in the emergence of apparently 'implicit' forms
and functions in current architecture; on the other hand, consideration of the issue of implicitness forms
a basis for new qualities, for new
spatial and constructive orders,
which appear 'simple', yet rational
and expedient.

The main intention behind the study of additive processes is to develop new constructive potentials and to realize these on an architectural scale. It was Gottfried Semper who demonstrated how different techni- cal archetypes developed in different cultures, not least through a 'pro- cess of transposition' or the application of different basic methods and uses to constantly new tools and procedures. Hence, the architectural result is always complex, influenced by different transformations, liber- ated or even emancipated from the original characteristic gesture of form and appearance by the transpositional process. However, according to Semper, despite all these influences and transformations, the different characteristics "that originate from the interaction of technology in a primitive architectural system", should eventually remain discernible.[4] This approach is exemplified by the project 'The Sequential Structure'[5] (12|1, 13|1 and 13|2), in which simple wooden slats are cut to length and then stacked freely by a robot: a traditional form of construction is embedded within a new technological environment and capable of adopting new manifestations by undergoing a transpositional process. This way, as opposed to the modular expression of addition, delicate structures with subtle transitions can be realised: plane surfaces merge seamlessly with curved ones, and an interaction between the rhythmic repetition of additively assembled wooden slats and their fine gradation in length is created. Moreover, the additive description of the system permits reacting to the load-bearing requirements of the structure, so that specifications with regard to design, structure, and manufacturing can be combined and optimised appropriately. This means, as illustrated by the functional clarity and constructive implicitness of 'The Sequential Structure'[6], that additive processes could play an important role in the digital age. Based on this method of construction, the tiniest units can form diverse groups, connections, and aggregations that simultaneously correspond to a digital and material logic. The question arises whether a central constructive moment should be proposed for current means of digital fabrication. Additive principles have always represented a deci- sive criterion in architecture and emerge anew within the current trans- fer to contemporary technologies: the modularity and uniformity of previous approaches is replaced by a complexity that aims at the actual constructive potential inherent in the particular material and leads to completely new forms of expression and meaning of additive structuring in architecture.[7]

Recursive and material-conscious design processes

Here, it becomes apparent that the greatest potential of digital materi- ality emerges where the number of individual components related to each other is particularly large. Even though these correlations are not incidental, but instead dependent upon each other and constitute each other according to particular rules, they comprise material structurings that can be interpreted in the sense of an open framework. This enables a system of dependencies, possibilities, and degrees of freedom through which digital architecture can enter into a new relationship with itself. This way, complex design processes can be developed that are directly dependent on the particular material employed, which could be associated with a material consciousness made accessible through digital methods. This also basically describes how material-conscious design processes should be understood and researched in the digital age of architecture. It encompasses an empirical, rather materialistic character of design, without which the relation to architectural research would remain an uninvolved 'process of information' detached from material and with no relation to architectural scale. As shown by the research activities at the Professorship Gramazio & Kohler, it is this 'exemplary' approximation to a constructive reality in the sense of real scale, real requirements, and real constructions that not only creates a prerequisite for architectural research in a digital age. It also enables description in linguistic terms, as well as access to material diversity.[8] Therefore, beyond traditional building materials, such as wood, brick, or concrete, it is also necessary to study 'structureless' materials such as sand or foam. Here, 'Procedural Landscapes' serves as an exemplary project[9] (6|1, 7|1 and 7|2). This project is based on procedural fabrication processes for the experimental design of landscapes, which are designed and materialised using a robot. Various aggregations of fine sand are created in an additive way. On the one hand, they display a high degree of complexity due to their material properties, and on the other hand, they can be repeated as often as required. Equipped with additional sensor technology, the robot enables the patterns created to be designed during the process of formation. This means that preexisting conical piles of sand are scanned and measurement data for further material accumulations are read so that quantity of sand, speed of motion, and drop height of new aggregations can be specifically adapted and manipulated: a recursive processuality is created that adapts again and again. It can be controlled systematically through programming, although the results obtained always contain an indeterminable component. Therefore, rather than achieving a materialisation of a particular geometrically predefined shape, the aim is to conduct a material-conscious study of design-relevant factors and structural properties during the process.

While experimental research in the 1970s was still completely focussed on 'natural constructions'[10] and similar landscape design methods, a highly interesting shift can be observed here: from material formation to digital fabrication and controlled design of such processes. Therefore, the project 'Procedural Landscapes' constitutes a highly important study

7

It would be interesting to also consider this in the context of a discussion on modules, building parts, and components. An increasing dynamisation with regard to complexity, variability, and functionality in architecture can be observed, not only concerning tools, but also building materials. Even though the architectural dispute on modularity and systemic building components represents a historically reconstructible, as well as tectonically relevant development, it is by no means settled conclusively. It may at best be noted that hierarchical modularisations and standardisations are in a process of dissolution and that completely new stabilities are articulated by the increasing technification of architecture. However, as shown by numerous research projects at the Professorship Gramazio & Kohler, this shift is less radical and explicit than often suggested, especially in contemporary discussions in architecture. The individualisation of building gains new freedom with regard to material, but this is always associated with new constraints and conventions, even though these may not appear to be immediately visible: streamlining of design processes, software applications, or also a standardisation of development and marketing processes. This inevitably leads to a return of standardisation. A new architectural need for normalisation and uniformity arises, especially in the digital age. This allows a shift from classical industrial paradigms on the material side, while at the same time permitting new standardisations and normalisations to be embraced on the immaterial, processual side. It is this 'dialectic of modularity' in the digital age that should be given new consideration in addition to the tool.

'The Sequential Structure'   **12|1**   realised pavilion

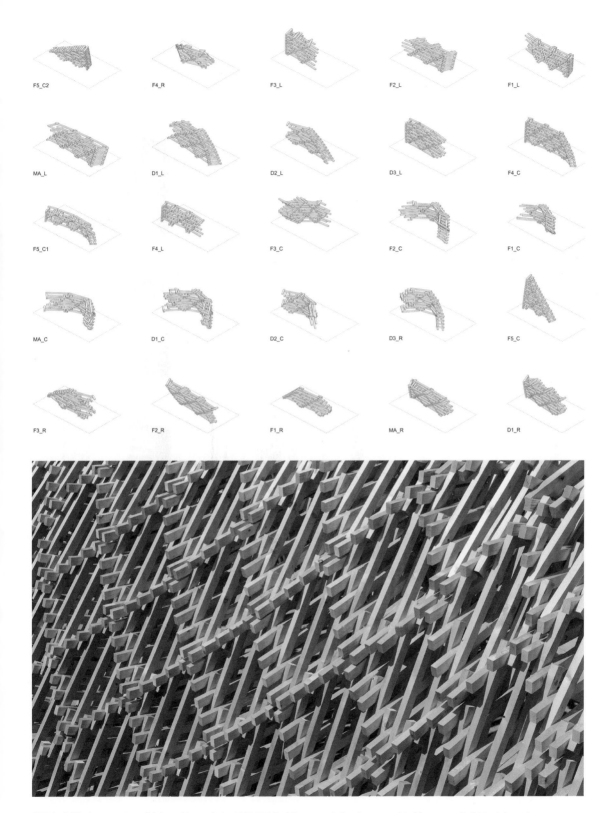

F5_C2   F4_R   F3_L   F2_L   F1_L

MA_L   D1_L   D2_L   D3_L   F4_C

F5_C1   F4_L   F3_C   F2_C   F1_C

MA_C   D1_C   D2_C   D3_R   F5_C

F3_R   F2_R   F1_R   MA_R   D1_R

13|1 Individual segments prefabricated by a robot   **13|2** Detail of the support structure assembled from many individual elements

8

With his comprehensively developed (political) association between artificial, social or natural spheres, the importance attributed by the French sociologist and philosopher Bruno Latour to a real ecology in the sense of a 'Dingpolitik' (politics of things) is on par with that of the culturally-representative or purely natural world. Cf.: Latour, Bruno: Politics of Nature. How to Bring Science into Democracy. Cambridge, MA 2004

9

The project 'Procedural Landscapes' is part of a course held at ETH Zurich in 2011 (project manager: Michael Knauss; students: Tobias Abegg, Jonathan Banz, Mihir Bedekar, Daria Blaschkiewitz, Simon Cheung, Dhara Dhara Sushil Surana, Felix Ernst, Hernan Garcia, Kaspar Helfrich, Pascal Hendrickx, Leyla Ilman, Malte Kloes, Jennifer Koschack, Caspar Lohner, Jitesh Mewada, Lukas Pauer, Sven Rickhoff, Martin Tessarz, Ho Kan Wong), supervised in collaboration with Prof. Christophe Girot, Institute of Landscape Architecture (ILA), ETH Zurich, and Yael Girot, Atelier Girot. This was made possible by establishment of an additional research facility including three modelling robots, allowing full integration of small-scale robot-based design and fabrication processes in academic teaching.

10

For example using approaches by Frei Otto regarding freely mobile, rolling material accumulations and conical piles capable of flowing using amorphous components such as sand and rubble. Cf.: Otto, Frei; Gass, Siegfried (ed.): 'IL25 Experimente.' [IL25 Experiments] Stuttgart 1990

that investigates intrinsic material behaviour in connection with digital fabrication methods and recursive design processes, while simultaneously transferring these to structureless materials.

This applies also if the created sand landscapes, or 'sandscapes', appear to comply with an assumed purely mechanical interpretation, reminiscent of more or less 'sequential' processes that allow the precise and apparently repetitive creation of free-form surfaces. However, on closer inspection, it becomes evident that the robot-created landscape aggregations display a degree of organisation that is essentially based on intrinsic material behaviour induced by robotic intervention. Its effects can – in contrast to earlier experiments in the 1970s – now be controlled, differentiated, and reproduced in their full complexity. Yet, they can't be drafted or modelled digitally or simulated in any other way. Despite this manifested complexity, the 'Procedural Landscapes' can be experienced intuitively and interpreted at different scales. Thus, the project addresses both human capacity to reflect procedural forms of organisation and to recognize singular momentariness.[11] Precisely such recursive and material-conscious design processes, in association with advanced digital fabrication processes, meet the challenge of diverse and complex material behaviour with all its aesthetic qualities. As result, the inclusion of open-end processes in digital fabrication becomes a decisive aspect.

Reflexive return of the machine

Perhaps it is this conceptual association of programming, additive forms of construction, and new material consciousness that bestows upon digital fabrication its particular expression and enables the robot to enter the discipline of architecture. As a 'multiple tool' it allows a diverse range of applications to be carried out quickly and precisely. But most of all, it enables working directly at the interface between digital and material spheres, thereby exercising a decisive influence on programming and design. Indeed, since the late 1980s the robot has, in fact, turned into an important tool in industrial and standardised forms of production. In a certain way, these were and are characteristic for the understanding of contemporary society and their inspiration for design-related disciplines throughout the 20th century. Paradoxically however, the development towards an increasingly reflexive, individual, and global 'stratification'[12] of cultural forms represents a further, even complementary 'turning point'[13] that explains why the robot, with its technified transformations and logical operations, is attributed more rather than less significance today: the robot not only has a command of a language of unity, but also a language of diversity.

Even though always latent in its 'DNS', the current emergence of this aspect turns the robot into a suitable tool not only in a standardised, but also in an individual and global production world: its 'generic' characteristics enable it to complete diverse tasks at a constant level of efficiency, precision, and flexibility, while remaining open for further adaptations and tasks. The same is valid for architecture: the robot gains its architectural significance through the fact that it facilitates the design of individual processes instead of uniform, standard products and realizes these on an architectural scale. Of equal importance is the fact that the additive forms of construction described here can be combined with the 'successive' constructive logic of robot-based manufacturing processes. This permits a direct synthesis of construction and robotics. As result, the robot combines the (old) world of industrial logic with the (new) world of the information age, thereby becoming a significant 'reflexive cultural form'. Since then, ranging between efficiency and precision, it has also become possible to meet the primacy of individualisation in technological terms. In contrast to industrial automation and the associated repetitive logic of continuously identical patterns, templates, and shapes, the task is now to advance the intrinsic 'skills' of the robot and to continuously increase its additive production potentials.

As previously mentioned, this means that the robot no longer predominantly operates within the typical spheres of industrial reproducibility characteristic for architecture for a long time, but in a real world with a rapidly increasing number of complex interactions – such as the interdependencies of data, construction, and fabrication central to this discussion. This is precisely where research at the Professorship Gramazio & Kohler sets in, providing an important contribution to architecture in its entirety, so that the previously merely marginal influence of digital technologies on architecture now gains a 'reflexive expression' through the robot, giving it seminal importance.

Paradoxical operationality of the robot

Navigating through this world with its altered circumstances of production, the question that repeatedly arises is why this task can't also be mastered without the robot. And in fact, when viewed globally, if it is easier for a craftsman to build a brick wall than for a robot, then – unless old paradigms of craftsmanship are to be meaninglessly perpetuated within the architectural discipline – something that could be called operationality of the robot applies at a specific level of complexity. Every material entity the modelling and qualification of which can only be provided by a robot becomes a justification of why the robot can do what man can't. This means that the robot develops its potential where an increasing number of complex relations and requirements suggests that human intervention is less practicable – both in quantitative and qualitative terms. Conversely, even though technically possible, it would not make much sense for robots to produce very simple building compo-

11

One of the issues described by the Spanish sociologist Manuel Castells is how new digital forms of organisation ('Space of Flows') are not only reflected in the typology, organisation, and representation of architecture and urban space, but also how perception and aesthetic significance can change into momentary emotions and processual reflections in this context. Cf.: Castells, Manuel: The Informational City. Information Technology, Economic Restructuring, and the Urban Regional Process. Oxford 1989

12

Beck, Ulrich; Giddens, Anthony; Lash, Scott: Reflexive Modernisation. Politics, Tradition and Aesthetics in the Modern Social Order. Cambridge 1994

13

It is commonly known that Konrad Wachsmann's 'Wendepunkt im Bauen' [Turning Point of Building] (1959) is rooted in a similar field; the same goes for work by Pier Luigi Nervi or Felix Candela. Wachsmann was a pioneer in his recognition of the effects of changes in industrial production on architectural design, and pre-empted these for the digital age. Within this 'Marxist' perspective, it is Wachsmann's differentiation between technology and architecture that is relevant to this discussion in the sense that the 'natural feeling for material and structure' postulated by Wachsmann appears to be rearticulated through the robot, as well as undergoing a renewed 'turning point' in the age of individual, digital producibility of architecture.

For the scope of individualisation trends cf. Industrialisation versus Individualisation » p. 24, Parametric Design Systems » p. 43, 52, Building Processes of Tomorrow » p. 128

16|1 **Transfer of the study results** of the 'Sequential Structure' to a robotic assembly of a roof truss within a wood research project

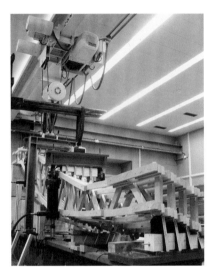

16|2 Successfully passed **stress test** of a robot-assembled truss

14

DeLanda, Manuel: A New Philosophy of Society. Assemblage Theory and Social Complexity. New York 2006

15

Carpo, Mario: Revolutions. Some New Technologies in Search of an Author. In: Log 15/2009

nents. In that case, the complexity essential for an architectural operationality of the robot is not applicable; aside from the fact that human labour based on craftsmanship skills on the one hand, and large-scale industrial automation on the other hand, offer far more efficient options for manufacturing simple, repetitive building components. Yet, the robot permits mastery of a much more complex world. This is less due to the interest in the 'technoid ontology' of the robot, but rather to something that is becoming increasingly visible in architecture today: the assembly of numerous complex, production-specific requirements and functions, as well as their individual implementation on a real scale.[14] This means that the 'degree of abstraction' typical for architecture is not applicable and that complexity can now be materialised more directly than ever before. Designs that were hardly feasible and made even less sense before the availability of the robot can now be designed easily and constructed with a robot.

This would mean that the major accomplishment resulting from the use of robots in architecture is the opportunity to reinterpret questions on efficiency, precision, and flexibility as a fundamental question on the practice and role of building. A significant aspect is – perhaps inconceivable for current lines of thought in architecture or even terminating in the often described dichotomy between man and machine – that approximating a comprehensive technological fabrication capacity as facilitated by the robot by no means corresponds to a devaluation of human diversity. On the contrary, human capabilities can be extended significantly through robot operationality. An improvement in the overview and control of complex material processes is achieved, but even more importantly, these can be implemented in a differentiated manner, and therefore, used for architectural purposes. Within this conceptual precondition, the robot is no longer restricted to the material world and its gravity or material properties, but also gains access to the immaterial world of thinking, design, and programming. According to the viewpoint of the Italian architectural historian Mario Carpo, this results in the disappearance of the separation between the act of design and the act of production, between man and machine, which has existed since the Renaissance. As result, the operationality of the robot can neither be limited to, nor excluded from material production processes, as well as the manner of how architecture is perceived intellectually, programmed, and designed.[15] Carpo's thesis gains analytical intensity when altered thus: that, in reverse, programming can be interpreted as an 'anthropological' form of design, construction, and materialisation. As result, the question can be raised whether the immanent logic of man and machine is visually manifested within the synthesis of programming and robot-assisted fabrication.

Technological advancedness and critical complexity

The fact remains that mankind is, by no means, relativised by the robot as cultural form, but assumes a leading role within a constructive reality ranging from programming to fabrication. The thus implied embrace of associative logic and anthropological craftsmanship could turn out to be so extensive in the future that this discussion would consequently have to focus on the opposite: by using the robot, mankind as author undergoes a profound reconceptualisation in the 'field of forces'[16] of the architectural information age. When, as demonstrated by the project 'Residential Building Eierbrechtstraße'[17] (18|1 and 18|2), an irregularly shaped building envelope composed of several thousand bricks is to be developed, this can no longer be realised with the grid patterns cultivated by man over centuries or with repeatable typologies. On the contrary: the facade of the multi-story residential building shows that the often complementary logic of brick course, window reveal, and building corner and roof line is less a question of the efficiency, precision, and flexibility facilitated by the robot. What is decisive is a fundamental way of dealing with architectural complexity and the ability to exemplify it, and thus, understanding it. Displacement of a single brick in the residential building in the Eierbrechtstraße, for example, changes an infinite number of relations between window positioning, brick courses, and the entire articulation of the building envelope. It is this architecturally complex interaction of complementary relationships and intentions that gains a new valorisation through the project: as a challenge for representation and simultaneous handling of numerous design- and fabrication-specific parameters. This requires new processes of decision-making, circumstances of implicitness, and degrees of freedom. It also encompasses the issue of 'controllability' to the extent that robot operationality could perhaps be met by a corresponding provision of human labour in required, yet vast quantities. However, it remains undisputed that this would mean less technological advancedness, and rather a return to a pre-industrial age. Even if permitted by social, cultural and political circumstances, this would not only be an economic problem, but also an ethical one. On the other hand, and preceding this, the robot offers an opportunity to develop a genuinely material-based understanding of design that is more than casually concerned with an efficient organisation of a specific quantity of building elements. Moreover, it becomes necessary to develop a comprehensive understanding of functional relationships and spatial dependencies, particularly in architectural terms. Contrary to common assumptions, the complexity facilitated by the use of the robot, and also demonstrated by projects such as the 'Residential Building Eierbrechtstraße', is not

16

Bourdieu, Pierre: 'Zur Soziologie der symbolischen Formen.' [On the Sociology of Symbolic Forms.] Frankfurt/M. 1997

17

The project 'Residential Building Eierbrechtstraße' by Gramazio & Kohler, Architecture and Urbanism is based on an ongoing research project by the Professorship Gramazio & Kohler (project manager: Tobias Bonwetsch) in collaboration with Keller AG Ziegeleien. The aim is to develop design software for individually articulated brick facades and simultaneous industrial realisation.

only limited to the pure tectonics of a building component or structure, but enables the unfolding of a comprehensive perspectivity of the material qualities of architecture.

Architectural enhancement of the rational and meaningful

In this study, robot-assembled structures are not only quantifiable as a whole, but each individual element has also become qualifiable, since it is possible to embed architectural information in a targeted manner. In this respect, the architectural substance of the robot lies in a process of differentiation of large quantities, which results in structure, i.e. in the control and further cultivation of excessive, unmanageable, and heterogeneous quantities. If these prerequisites are fulfilled, robot-assembled structures are characterised by an unusually large quantity of elements that are organised in detail, a high degree of constructive precision, and simultaneous presence of complex links between the entire structure and individual elements. This not only changes the architectural design and its realisation, but also the architectural expression, as exemplified by the projects 'Residential Building Eierbrechtstraße', 'The Sequential Structure' or 'Procedural Landscapes', and demonstrated by 'The Programmed Column' (19|1 and 19|2). Here, architecture appears technologically alien, yet materially familiar, simultaneously permitting manifold connections between craftsmanship and technology, between man and machine.

Therefore, the following provisional statement can be made: beyond a rational and expedient evaluation, the robot is a fascinating instrument in architecture in the digital age, precisely because it allows discovering new, multi-layered forms of organisation far beyond any kind of determinism. As result, new insight for further discoveries may be gained. However, it remains to be seen how robots will develop in future. Yet, what should be taken into account at this point is that the operationality of data and material is certainly not merely a subject of digital aesthetics; it is far more than a short-lived chapter of the digital age. Instead, it can be considered as a perspectivity that allows an open, diverse, and tangible enhancement of architecture within a particular and technologically based mode of observation, from computer programming to fabrication with the industrial robot. This not only permits study and inclusion of the latest universal technologies within the practice of the discipline, but also allows interrelating these developments in a spatial and material context, and as result, utilising them in cultural terms.

18|1 Computer-generated detail of a facade study of the **'Residential Building Eierbrechtstraße'**

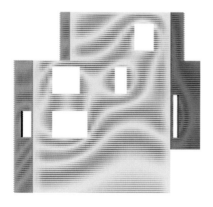

18|2 Image of the **interference patterns** on the facade of the 'Residential Building Eierbrechtstraße'

19|1 and 19|2 **'The Programmed Column'** project and its physical structuring of bricks to form a vertical supporting structure

Industrialisation versus Individualisation – New Methods and Technologies

Text   Petra von Both

In order to overcome the ongoing economic problems that the building industry is faced with, a significant increase in both the efficiency and the effectiveness of construction processes is necessary. However, a closer examination makes it clear that the building industry worldwide has fallen well behind in comparison with other industries in terms of innovation and the use of future-oriented methods and technologies.

A study by the American National Institute of Building Science (NIBS) very clearly indicates the negative development of the productivity index within the building industry over the past 40 years and illustrates the need to reassess existing processes and methods, as well as the technical instruments used.[1]

In the USA, striking improvements have been achieved in recent years in terms of efficiency in planning and manufacturing through the effective use of computers in the planning and building process, as well as through the application of industrial manufacturing and assembly methods.[2] In contrast, the German building industry finds itself in a state of increasingly intense competition within the global context.

As chambers of architects and engineers have now recognised, the cause of this situation lies in a working methodology that is often inefficient and tied to outdated methods and role models.[3] However, responses to

1

Zentralverband Deutsches Bauge-werbe e. V. (ed.): Analysis & Forecast. Building Industry Report 2010/2011. Berlin 2011

2

Young, Norbert W.; Bernstein, Harvey M.: Key Trends in the Construction Industry. Smart Market Report: Design & Construction Intelligence. Study commissioned by McGraw-Hill Construction. New York 2006

3

Hommerich, Christoph; Ebers, Thomas: Analysis of the Costs and Earnings Situation in Architectural Practices. Results of a Represen-tative Survey commissioned by the Federal Chamber of Architects. Bergisch Gladbach 2006

this situation consist, for the most part, as an increased specialisation and division of work within the planning and building process in order – in the Taylorist tradition – to achieve a reduction in complexity and increased efficiency within the individual processes through segmentation. However, in most cases this results in an isolated sequential handling of the processes, leading to quality loss due to increased problems of compatibility between the separately optimised partial solutions.

Therefore, a solution can only be found in an increase in the global added value, i.e. in this context relating to the project as a whole. Experts assume that an increase in productivity can, in particular, be achieved through innovation and integration within the planning and building process, through the use of new integrated technologies, computer-based 3D/4D modelling of structures, linking of CAD and CAM technologies, and the development of new processes, as well as new types of services.[4] Another current topic is the question on how much a more extensive industrialisation of production within the field of construction would benefit the building industry in Europe and the German building industry in particular. Whether and how approaches adopted from the consumer goods industry, for example mass production, can be transferred to the building industry, and which alternative technological and methodical solutions exist will be discussed in the following.

The law of mass production

The law of mass production expresses the relationship between the costs of a production method and the quantity of the product that is produced.[5] The German economist Karl Bücher first formulated the effects associated with this principle in 1910.[6] He established that unit costs fall with increasing production quantities, since the fixed costs are spread across a greater quantity of units (economies of scale). Therefore, in the case of more capital-intensive production methods, it is advantageous to produce greater quantities.[7] However, it has also been found that technical advances lead to production methods requiring an increasingly high initial investment. In order to practise mass production successfully, mass consumption is necessary: increasing fixed costs necessarily encourage a tendency towards large-scale production.[8]

An application of these principles to the building industry requires corresponding large-scale organisational structures. However, a glance at current practice reveals a very fine-grained organisational structure on the part of both planners and builders:[9]

- 92 percent of companies in the construction industry employ fewer than 20 individuals.
- The average size of engineering and architectural practices currently ranges from three to five individuals.

Concerning further aspects of the integration of planning, construction, and manufacturing processes, see also » *p. 25 as well as The Operationality of Data and Material* » *p. 9, Material, Information, Technology* » *p. 31, Parametric Design Systems* » *p. 43, Construction Processes of the Future* » *p. 126*

4

Bernstein, Harvey M.: The Business Value of BIM. Smart Market Report: Design & Construction Intelligence. European study commissioned by McGraw-Hill Construction. New York 2009

5

University of Erlangen-Nürnberg, Institute of Economics: Online textbook, chapter 5. Control Processes. The Rationalisation Principle. http://www.economics.phil.uni-erlangen.de/bwl/lehrbuch/kap5/rational/rational.pdf (accessed on 04.08.2011)

6

König, Wolfgang: History of the Consumer Society. Stuttgart 2000

7

The Law of Mass Production. In: Wirtschaftslexikon24.net (accessed on 05.08.2011)

8

Molsberger, Josef: Economies of Scale? On the Thesis of the Inevitability of Economic Concentration. Abhandlungen zur Mittelstandsforschung 31. Cologne 1967

9

Federal Office of Statistics (ed.): Statistical Yearbook 2009 for the Federal Republic of Germany. Wiesbaden 2009; see note 4

22|1 fg 2000, Altenstadt (D) 1968,
Wolfgang Feierbach

10

Le Corbusier: The Modulor. A harmonious measure to the human scale universally applicable to architecture and mechanics. Stuttgart 1978

11

see note 6

In 1850 the French author Théophile Gautier wrote: "Humanity will produce a completely new type of architecture as soon as new methods developed by industry are applied."

Iken, Katja: Instant Dream Living Spaces. In: einestages – Zeitgeschichten in SpiegelOnline (accessed on 10.01.2011)

12

see note 6, p. 67

13

Cobbers, Arnt; Jahn, Oliver: Prefab Houses. Cologne 2010

Such organisational structures are particularly prevalent in the area of individual project business, where a focus on core competencies guarantees survival within the increasingly internationalised market. However, such segmentation and isolated optimisation of the functions impedes optimisation of the process as a whole, due to lacking design of interfaces. What is needed, then, are adequate business models and processes, which allow efficiency and productivity to be increased within the existing organisational structures. Mass production approaches can only be applied to certain manufacturers of building components and prefabricated parts, and only within the framework of practical levels of standardisation.

The topic of standardisation is not new: this issue was much discussed among architects within the Modernist movement in particular, and numerous solutions, some very prominent, were developed. For example, one could mention AFNOR (Association française de normalisation), founded in 1926, as well as the association ASCORAL (Assemblée de Constructeurs pour Rénovation architecturale), founded by Le Corbusier in 1940, both of which were concerned with standardisation and industrial fabrication methods.[10]

Prefabricated houses and system building

Standardisation approaches on a comprehensive building-related scale were and continue to be applied in the field of prefabricated houses. The industrial production of large quantities of identical products using standardised individual components and assemblies makes it possible to create living space for large numbers of people in an economical way.[11] This idea led to initial applications of mass production to the building industry, which already appeared at the time of the industrial revolution, with the pioneering spirit of this era encouraging a very positive reception of such approaches.

In the 1920s various attempts were made to use concrete as building material – due to its homogeneity, more suitable for use in mass production than heterogeneous timber products – as the basis for prefabricated housing modules. However, in the view of technology historian Wolfgang König these attempts were unsuccessful because the "designs and execution of concrete houses" proved "unsatisfactory".[12]

The housing shortage following the Second World War led to a renaissance in the concept of the prefabricated house, with many companies formerly involved in the defence sector and aircraft construction moving into the market. One example of this is the so-called Vultee house developed by the Vultee Aircraft Corporation (1947). This building, assembled from 28 prefabricated sheet metal components, shows very clear references to existing manufacturing technologies and known materials.[13] With the development of new materials, the 1970s saw a trend towards the plastic house. One example of this is the house "fg 2000" by Wolfgang Feierbach (22|1) from the year 1968. Prefabricated fibreglass modules permitted rapid assembly without any need for cranes or lifting gear.[14] The international plastic house exhibition "ika 71" in Lüdenscheid in 1971 constituted the apex in the brief career of the often futuristic free-form buildings made of plastic, designed above all for use as holiday homes.[15] From the 1980s onwards, the building industry increasingly turned to construction methods that permitted individualisation, which meant that the concept of the prefabricated house tended to fade into the background – often also due to the deficient properties of the buildings in terms of building physics.

However, the economic crisis of recent years has shifted the focus of interest back towards the idea of the economical prefabricated house, also from a viewpoint of cost certainty. Yet, this requires that characteristics regarding energy efficiency and sustainability of modern prefabricated houses, which mostly comprise timber construction, are already known from the onset. Still, despite a growth of approximately 10 percent in the year 2010 the market share of prefabricated houses remains at a comparatively low level of roughly 15 percent.[16]

A significantly more flexible approach than that offered by prefabricated houses is represented by system building. This involves a standardisation not of the overall structure, but of the components and methods used. The advantages of this approach lie in the improved adaptability and configurability of the systems, as well as in the relatively short assembly time at the construction site. Moreover, the separation in space and time of component manufacture and assembly on the building site allows complete independence from weather conditions during the prefabrication phase. Further, it also allows a high degree of precision to be achieved in the often mass-produced building components.

Probably one of the most consistent implementations of this approach was by Fritz Haller. In addition to developing the well-known flexibly expandable and reconfigurable furniture system USM Haller, he was responsible for various modular systems for building and also applied his design principles to urban planning projects with social and utopian orientation.

On the level of individual buildings, he was concerned with the development of different functional system typologies that, while embracing the concept of flexibility, also permitted meeting the requirements of specific usages. This led to the development of three so-called modular building systems, which also allow a highly flexible and efficient integration of building utilities, in addition to their precisely elaborated structural design (23|1):

- USM Haller MINI for residential and office buildings
- USM Haller MIDI for buildings with high degree of installation, such as schools or laboratories
- USM Haller MAXI for industrial structures

14

ibid.

15

see note 13

16

Bundesverband Deutscher Fertigbau e. V.: Economic Situation of the German Prefab Industry. http://www.bdfev.de/german/verband/wirtschaft/index.html (accessed on 05.08.2011)

23|1 Application of a Modular System, Expansion of the Cantonal School, Solothurn (CH) 1997, Fritz Haller

Concerning the scope of tendencies towards individualisation, see The Operationality of Data and Material » *p. 15*, *Parametric Design Systems* » *p. 43*, *52, Construction Processes of the Future* » *p. 128*

17

http://insm.de/insm/Aktionen/ Lexikon/i/Individualisierung.html (accessed on 05.08.2011)

18

ibid.

This diversification of target groups is now also being seen within the field of urban development that, by targeted use of milieu studies (for example by the Sinus Institute, http://www.sinus-institut.de/loesungen/sinus-milieus. html, accessed on 05.08.2011), in addition to age and income structures, also uses equally group-specific socio-cultural aspects and value systems as a basis for planning.

19

Piller, Frank T.: Mass Customization. A Strategic Concept for Competition in the Information Age. Wiesbaden 2006

20

Dörflinger, Markus; Marxt, Christian: Mass Customization – New Potential through Customer Specific Mass Production (I). Combination of Efficient Mass Production with Customer-specific Individual Production. In: io Management, 03/2001

However, similarly as the prefabricated house, the modular system approach tended to be pushed into the background during the phase of individualisation – especially in the field of residential building – that began in the 1980s.

Individualisation and mass customisation

Individualisation can be observed in both socio-cultural and economic terms. In the 1980s the sociologist Ulrich Beck contributed substantially to this topic, which also plays an important role in the discussion relating to social change within modern society, involving a "dissolution of traditional ways of living, lifestyle norms and behavioural orientations"[17]. One important aspect here is the individualisation of the value system: from an economic viewpoint, individualisation can also be seen as a "trademark and competitive factor".[18] An improved focus on customers on the part of corporations, combined with precisely specified market and target group orientation of products and services enables providing products that are individually tailored to customers.

Developed in recent years and related to above described processes, the approach of "mass customisation"[19] attempts to combine the advantages of individual manufacture with the principles of mass production. The idea behind this is to serve a relatively large market and simultaneously be able to take into account individual customer requirements without exceeding the costs of standard products. This is achieved through an increase in the diversity of available variants, as well as more efficient customer-specific product development through improved planning and manufacturing. The aim is to place individual products in mass markets, while costs remain stable or even decline.[20] In order to achieve this, modern production technologies are combined with the principles of e-commerce. But how can this approach be applied to the building industry?

Individualised system building

Individualised system building attempts to expand the planning freedom that is generally limited by consequently employing a systematised modular building system. It aims to achieve this by combining standardised system components with individual details in order to create customer-specific solutions. However, the disadvantages of limited individual planning solutions associated with system building cannot be fully compensated by this rather configuration-based approach.

Still, such an approach, when based on parameterisable components, can be suitable for renovation projects, and particularly energy-efficiency modernisation. Figure 25|1 shows the elementisation and parameterisation of a thermal insulation composite system realised as part of the

EISAN research project at the University of Karlsruhe, as well as the subsequent automated manufacture and assembly based on an individual measurement and topological analysis of buildings.

Automated one-off production

Another highly promising approach for the efficient project-specific development of one-off products is automated manufacture, also referred to as CAD/CAM integration (Computer-Aided Design/Computer-Aided Manufacturing). A prerequisite for this is an integrated planning and manufacturing process based on CAx technologies. This requires the existence of a complete digital, and thus, validatable description of the planning object by means of a virtual building model (Building Information Modelling – BIM), which can represent the various structural, functional, and technical aspects, as well as manufacturing-related constraints. The BIM then serves as data reference for later manufacture.[21]

Numerous studies show that it is possible to create a considerable added value through the increased use and further development of this integrated BIM approach.[22] Studies in the USA indicate savings potentials of up to 50 percent in terms of time and costs with effective use of BIM and also make it clear that the additional costs resulting from insufficient interoperability in construction projects in the USA account for approximately 4.3 percent of total costs. This is equivalent to an annual cost factor of 15.8 billion dollars in the USA alone.[23]

The buzzword "virtual engineering" refers to the development and application of a model-based planning methodology rooted in an expanded BIM approach. However, this relates not only to the interlinking of the software used; the interface to digital scanning tools, output media, and visualisation media also plays an important role. The aim is to create a continuous process from the real object context to the virtual planning model and combined CAD and CAM technologies, as well as rapid prototyping (RP).

Within the building industry, this integrated BIM approach to linking planning and manufacture has primarily been adopted in practice by the larger general contractors and coordinating contractors, since these are able to exploit a high added value. This is due to the high degree of continuity within their own in-house processes. In addition to a considerable increase in efficiency, adherence to deadlines, and cost certainty, this also leads to a significant improvement in product quality. In steel construction, for example, tolerances of less than 0.1 millimetres can be achieved through systematic CAD-CAM control of the manufacturing machines.[24] Particularly in infrastructure projects where quality is critical, such as the construction of rapid transit rail lines, the use of CAD/CAM can become a decisive competitive factor. In concrete construction, the com-

Concerning further aspects of the integration of planning, construction, and manufacturing processes, see also » *p. 21 as well as The Operationality of Data and Material* » *p. 9, Material, Information, Technology* » *p. 31, Parametric Design Systems* » *p. 43, Construction Processes of the Future* » *p. 126*

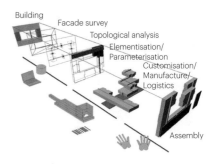

25|1 Parametric planning as a basis for individual scalability

21

Both, Petra von: Integrated Product Lifecycle Management. Strategies for achieving a continuous process integration in the building industry. In: Verband deutscher Ingenieure: VDI Yearbook 2008. Düsseldorf 2007

22

Maisberger Whiteoaks: New Business Potential for Architects and Engineers. Study commissioned by Nemetschek AG. Munich 2005; see note 2

23

Gallaher, Michael P. et al.: Cost Analysis of Inadequate Inter-Operability in the U.S. Capital Facilities Industry. U.S. Department of Commerce, Technology Administration, National Institute of Standards and Technology. Gaithersburg, MD 2004

Schreyer Markus: BIM and Working
Processes in Project Management.
Possibilities offered by Partnering.
Neumarkt 2008. http://www.building-
smart.de/pdf/BIM-Anwendertag-
Schreyer.pdf (accessed on 10.01.2011)

26|1 and 26|2 Student Project involving a
3-axis low-cost self-made milling machine
at the Karlsruhe Institute for Technology

25

Koch, Volker et al.: One Mill per
Student. Designing a Low Cost Pro-
totype Mill for Architectural Use.
In: Conference Transcript of the 28th
eCAADe Conference. Zurich 2010

puter-aided methodology described above facilitates a highly economical manufacture of complex individual geometries. In the field of parametric free-form modelling, these methods can, for example, be used to
assist the implementation of current architectural trends.

Outlook: low-cost approach and on-site manufacture

As described, the methods of automated one-off production offer considerable potential for increasing efficiency, quality, and cost certainty in
construction and infrastructure projects. Supplemented by the use of
new IT-aided technologies and methods in the field of planning, prepara-
tion, logistics, and the execution of construction work, these allow considerable improvements to be achieved throughout the entire planning
and building process.

However, the degree of technical upgrading required by the production
method requires a level of investment that should not be underestimated, which is why the methods of integrated CAD/CAM technology
and rapid prototyping have so far and for the most part been available
only to larger companies. Due to the finely-divided organisational structure within the building industry, further expenditure on development
and research is, therefore, necessary to allow this approach to be adopted
on a broader basis. In relation to the investment budgets available to the
different participants in the building process, the Department of Building Lifecycle Management (BLM) of the Karlsruhe Institute for Technology is working on the development of a low-cost approach in the area of
rapid prototyping. For example, a project conducted with students indicated that a low-cost 3-axis milling machine with a precision sufficient
even for architectural modelling, including software, can be made avail-
able for less than 2000 euros (26|1 and 26|2).[25]

In general, it is to be expected that future cost reduction, as well as the
significantly increasing technical sophistication of RP technologies will
make these methods more and more accessible to smaller companies.
With the reduction in costs and anticipated wider availability of RP systems, future research should also inquire on whether these systems and
equipment will need to stay in the workshop, or can be used directly on
site as a mobile tool. The advantages of moving these tools to the building site are obvious: the transport logistics are greatly simplified, trans-
port-related damage of building components can be avoided, and it
becomes possible to respond directly and immediately to unforeseeable
events on the building site. The relocation of production processes to the
building site can prove particularly effective if they are preceded by a precise and rapid 3D measuring method, and significant time savings combined with a high quality of workmanship can be achieved through a
direct combination of measuring, diagnosis, planning, and manufacture.

Especially when carrying out structural renovations during operation, extremely effective planning and manufacturing processes become possible that impact users only to a minimal degree. For example, such a method has significant advantages when it comes to modernising building utilities, since it is often impossible to carry out a preemptive diagnosis of wall layers and technical systems that are not directly accessible when conducting renovation during operation. In this case, the method of on-site measuring and manufacture permits efficient, problem-oriented planning and application to be carried out while renovation work takes place.

This methodological approach is not restricted to specific building tasks, but is applicable to different scenarios and building materials. In cooperation with a building materials manufacturer, work is currently being carried out on further developing a concept involving aerated concrete as construction material.

Figure 27|1 shows the principle of integrated measurement, planning, and manufacture applied to the scenario of restoration of a listed facade: first, 3-D scanning data are recorded and analysed to produce manufacturing data for the frieze element that is to be replaced. The 3-axis milling machine that is located on site is used to create a perfect-match replica, which can then be inserted directly in the area of damage.

In addition to technological innovations, the future relocation of such planning services to the building site or to the contractors carrying out the work will require a rethinking of existing tendering and contract structures. For this reason, the focus of ongoing research work at the Department of Building Lifecycle Management will not simply remain on technological levels, but also on the level of the processes and organisational framework conditions that are subject to change due to the implementation of such technologies.

27|1 **Automated Restoration:** Laser-aided Measurement, Manufacture, and Assembly

28|1 The **'Plopp'** aluminium stool has such low weight that it can be suspended from a helium balloon. Exhibit at the furniture trade fair in Milan in 2011

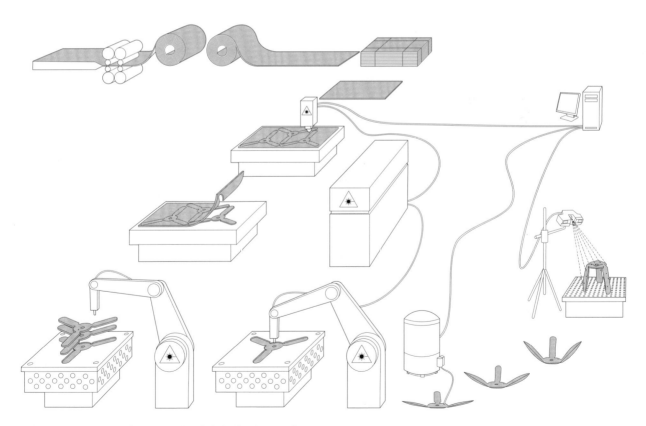

29|1 Schematic structure of the **production chain** for the 'Plopp' stool

Material, Information, Technology – Options for the Future

Text Philipp Dohmen, Oskar Zieta

The future will be shaped by a number of different aspects: a sensitivity towards wastage of materials and energy, the increasing individualisation of society, as well as the demands of our information age. We will continue to remain dependent on technology, perhaps even more so than in the past. It is exciting to see how tasks of combining technology and information are becoming increasingly easy; the actual challenge lies in the fact that materials need to be 'in-formed', i.e. brought into a particular form. As long as information is merely virtual and doesn't actually bring anything 'into form', it is without value. To understand the interplay between material, information, and technology we must examine the processes that bring these together. It is these that require development.

Material

The material that Oskar Zieta and Philipp Dohmen have been trying to 'inform' for more than ten years is metal, more precisely sheet metal. Sheet metal is an important building material that has become well established in the field of architecture in the 20th century, especially as a cladding material, due to the application of industrial processing methods. As a rolled semifinished product of relatively low thickness, sheet metal is a widely used material with which high-precision products can be implemented to a high technological standard. Here, the mechanical engineering industries, and the automotive industry in particular, are drivers of innovation in research and development. In this sector, the development of computer-controlled processing methods in the past 20 years has triggered a real surge in innovation. Particular importance is thereby attached to the material properties of sheet metal. For example, forming processes can turn the material into an extremely robust form and produce light and extremely stable constructions. Although metals are readily recyclable, they are a finite resource. Therefore, they will become increasingly expensive over the course of time, which is why the economical use of material is becoming increasingly important as well – not least in order to save energy.

Information

The information used for the process of forming is optimised for information-technology-based methods. It is derived in part from simulations, but for the most part from empirical investigations. Information always communicates a difference and loses its quality as soon as it has performed its informing function. The key aspect is its property of causing changes in the receiving system. Our interest lies in using information to bring about loss-free changes through processes, and to control these in such a way that allows us to transpose objects from the virtual realm seamlessly into reality. Innovative industrial production methods were studied systematically for several years at the faculty of Computer-Aided Architectural Design (CAAD) at the ETH Zurich under Prof. Ludger Hovestadt. The aim of this research was the development of computer-aided design and building processes, as well as the digitisation of the associated interfaces. The computer is able to calculate and control production and design processes that involve numerous parameters. The resulting 'digital chain' describes an uninterrupted digital process from design through design engineering up to production, which allows significant freedom in designing. Information-based production forms of sheet metal permit both more complex constructions and significantly smaller series – even as so-called one-of-a-kind production. This development is particularly interesting for architecture, since it offers the possibility of an industrial and economical manufacture of building elements. At this point in time, architecture benefits from CNC-based connection and design solutions adopted from the field of mechanical engineering that are transferred to an architectural scale and interpreted anew. These new technical possibilities also contribute to the current development of free forms in building.

31|1 The **laser welding installation** completes a 9 metre long weld in 45 seconds, FiDU element for the 'SeaHorse' project
31|2 **Laser welding robot** for FiDU elements

Concerning further aspects of the integration of planning, building, and manufacturing processes, see also The Operationality of Data and Material » *p. 9, Industrialisation versus Individualisation* » *p. 21, 25, Parametric Design Systems* » *p. 43, Construction Processes of the Future* » *p. 126*

Computerised Numerical Control (CNC) *"Computerised Numerical Control" is an electronically based method for controlling and regulating machine tools. It allows several processing steps to be performed on a workpiece through programmable tool movements. A high precision and high speed of manufacture can be achieved using CNC machines.*

Technology

The technology used in sheet metal processing is a combination of processing methods that focus on flexibility in terms of three main working steps: separating, joining, and forming.

The first object or rather product of the experimentation with different processing methods in 2001 was a pavilion (32|1 and 32|2). This built manifesto relied on the effective utilisation of a machine that is capable of manufacturing one-off products: the laser cutter. The laser is a tool- and contact-free, very readily informable separating method. Laser cutting allows virtually any shape to be cut, even complicated and delicate forms, from thin sheet metal up to 30 millimetre thick, coarse sheet metal panels (31|1). Thus, the laser constitutes the perfect tool for one-off products and small series of up to 10,000 items per annum. Since the technology is under continuous development, the costs are continually falling, which means that the number of running metres cut per minute is becoming increasingly economical, and thus more attractive. This development is comparable with the leap forward from the printing machine to the laser printer. Whereas, due to high initial costs, a printing machine only really functions cost-effectively at large print runs, the initial costs with a laser printer are zero, and each page costs the same amount, even if it is printed differently. Similarly, with the laser the automated control means that it makes no difference whether it cuts out 100 different parts or 100 identical parts. In the case of the pavilion, this involved approximately 500 different parts, and a glance at the 500 cutting patterns (37|2) makes it clear that it seems more sensible to automate such a process, since manual processing would quickly lead to a loss of oversight. In order to control the individual parts, a program was developed that can virtually display these per roll in completed form at the touch of a button. These cutting patterns were then transferred to the actual sheet metal. The very simple system of interconnections used in the pavilion indicates that this enabled producing a flat surface just as easily as a double-curved surface or a corner by using a single system. The result was a unique tube-like form 4 metres in length and 3 metres in diameter – the first ever architectural project to be realised within a continuous digital chain.

Preferably, the laser is also used for joining, in this case through welding, which requires a somewhat different technique (31|2). Heat conduction welding, the most commonly used method along with TIG and CMT welding, produces narrow welds with minimal distortion at high speeds. As a CNC joining tool, it is the perfect method for this application: it is tool- and contact-free and ideally suitable for one-off products and small series.

We have been testing different possible techniques for metal forming for a long time. In continuing the experimental technological deliberation

32|1 Detail of the **SxM pavilion**, consisting of automatically generated N- and Z-shaped sheet metal elements
32|2 The **SxM pavilion** was the first project to assume the form of a digital chain, developed and built in 2001 by postgraduate students at the CAAD faculty of the ETH Zurich.

on the material, we systematically investigated complex deformation processes. Traditionally, metal forming is carried out using deep drawing and bending machines. However, only linear deformations are possible with universal forming tools; moreover, closed profiles can only be produced with difficulty. The aim was to develop practices that reduce the design and functional practices involved in the processing of sheet metal to a minimum. So-called hydroforming is one such process of deformation. With this method, originally developed in the automobile industry, tubes are formed by high pressure. However, the size of the parts to be produced also essentially depends on the dimensions of the tool. This means that it is almost impossible to use this method to produce elements suitable for architectural applications, i.e. story-height elements. Forming with extremely high pressures of up to 12,000 bar is very energy-intensive. Moreover, there are only a few production locations in Europe. The associated tool costs quickly run into millions, and generally only large production runs guarantee returns for such costs. However, in the field of architecture and design, this represents an exclusion criterion: in the building industry, 1000 identical elements are already considered a large production run, yet they would never lead to recovering costs.

A further technological development of this method was achieved through 'a step backwards'. For lack of access to hydroforming production facilities and for cost reasons, two items were omitted: high pressure and the expensive tool. The resulting method, so-called free internal pressure forming (Freie-Innen-Druck-Umformung or FiDU), offers the advantages of enabling sheet metal to be processed without requiring any tools. The form is determined solely by the geometry of the pre-cut element, the material, its thickness, and the internal pressure applied. First, the contours of the metal sheets are cut out with the laser, then two metal sheets are placed tightly together and welded along the edge. The movement sequences of the robot are controlled directly via the computer. The subsequent inflation of the welded shapes is achieved by introducing water or air into the cavity. The duration and the pressure of between 0.2 and 50 bar determine the degree of alteration of the metal sheets. After the pressure has been released, the form that has been achieved is retained. While using the same amount of material, the resulting product is many times more stable than comparable forms manufactured from canted sheet metal elements. Within static load tests, statics predictions were exceeded beyond expectations (33|1).

In addition to sheet steel, this method can serve to form brass, copper, and aluminium. Of course, the potential of aluminium for the manufacture of ultra-lightweight constructions is even greater. When lifting up a FiDU element made of aluminium, the typical expectation of the object's mass to weight relation is surprisingly turned on its head (34|2).

The two steps of laser cutting and welding are regarded as being highly precise. For this reason, reservations as to whether this accuracy might

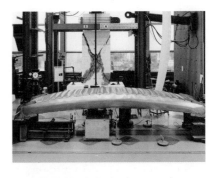

33|1 **FiDU bridge** before load testing in the testing hall at the ETH Zurich

An impressive loading test *was carried out with a 6 metre long bridge made of 1 millimetre thick steel sheet metal* (33|1). *With a dead weight of only 170 kilograms, the stress analysts and structural engineers expected it to withstand maximum loads of no more than 300 kilograms. The bridge finally gave way at a load of 1.8 tonnes; the process was clearly recognisable and gradual, as is desirable in the failure of load-bearing structures. The ratio of dead weight to load-bearing capacity was thus greater than 1:10. Thus, despite the mundane and economical material used, this places it in the category of ultra-lightweight constructions.*

34|1 **Scanning of a FiDU element** in order to measure deviations resulting from the manufacturing process. In this case, the maximum deviation is 0.6 millimetres.

34|2 3 metre long **FiDU element** that connects three points in space and weighs less than 20 kilograms.

not be entirely lost through the inflation process led to a project involving numerous identical and extremely precise parts. The 4 metres wide FiDU football, fittingly presented to coincide with Euro 2008 in Switzerland, consists of a truncated icosahedron with 90 edges (38|1). Each deviation within the millimetre range would have made closing the structure impossible. Series of 100 objects that only differ within the range of half a millimetre have since been measured in scientific studies (34|1). Thus, a forming method supposedly lacking in precision emerges as sufficiently precise to be suitable for series production – and therefore, more than sufficiently accurate for building applications.

FiDU is a processing method that effectively continues the freedom and potential offered by laser cutting and welding into the forming process, resulting in stable and precise elements. Moreover, the method also allows non-linear and complex alterations of forms to be achieved. These deformations, correlated to the properties of sheet metal, lead to a formal language not previously associated with the material. Thus, a completely new perspective on the material within the field of architecture emerges. Both the range of possible processing technologies and the physical properties of the material were investigated in different experiments. The rules of metal forming were researched in detail and the findings integrated in the design process. The key is to select the material processing parameters for cutting and inflating the material in such a way that the final form corresponds exactly to the design idea. And the 'die' used is nothing more than air. If parameters are mastered appropriately, FiDU can expand the range of tool- and contact-free technologies available for one-off products and small series.

For the future, this means that individual, yet complex elements can be manufactured simply; elements that are light, yet also stable, and thus save material and energy. However, statements of this kind inevitably come with a caveat: this is only possible if one adopts the semantics of the FiDU alphabet.

The FiDU alphabet

Our research was aimed at a production run of one. Hydroforming was not an affordable option, but the idea of forming something from the inside remained very attractive. The results of initial experiments with FiDU were astounding. Several millimetre-thick sheets of stainless steel were transformed into remarkable, wrinkled cushion-like forms simply by water pressure. After a number of such cushions had been produced, some critics dismissed these as 'bent scrap'. However, a number of experiments revealed astonishingly precise bends and curvatures that were repeatable and led to consistent, symmetrical elements. Since there were no rules, no literature, and no references on such deformations to follow, based on learning by doing we first had to make all kinds of mistakes in order to learn from these. During the course of many courses and numerous experiments, we built up a database of deformation rules, which were derived from the objects. We refer to this collection of forming rules as the FiDU alphabet. It consists of letters representing individual aspects of how a two-dimensional form will behave three-dimensionally under the influence of internal pressure. Lining up letters creates words, the combination of which, in turn, produces sentences. In the courses taught at the ETH Zurich, this required a change of mindset from the students. Having to learn letters in order to express something didn't exactly match their notions of creative design; however, the sheet metal was unyielding, and in every instance would only deform in accordance with these rules identified by letters. As with language – anyone who has mastered the rules and can arrange the letters skilfully is able to use these to compose a poem. And who would deny that writing poetry is a creative act?

The first three letters: Plopp

One successful poem created with the FiDU alphabet is certainly the 'Plopp' stool (28|1 and 29|1). It consists of only three letters, i.e. three rules. Put briefly, the first letter P states that round forms can be inflated evenly, whereas sharp angles cannot. The letter L stands for the useful opening in the stool's centre that allows gripping it comfortably. Stools aren't actually ideally designed for sitting on, so it is quite interesting to experience for oneself the surprisingly comfortable seat surface of the 'Plopp'. The rule also states that things can be inflated to an equal extent if they share the same width, which means that the legs are as wide as the ring of the seat surface. This creates the bulging curves on all sides. In turn, the rule O stands for the ultimately complex aspect of this simple piece of furniture: the crease. It states that the contours need to be narrowed at the point at which a crease is to be created. The radii that describe this narrowing lead to the reproducibly precise creases, which are the actual secret of the 'Plopp'. During deformation, their proximity along the inner fold allows all legs to move until they are inclined at almost 70 degrees (35|2). The crease itself is so exact that a precise protrusion is formed every time, which in return fits into the indent on the opposite side and gives the stool its extraordinary stability (38|2). During the inflation process, the precise indents in the seat surface are formed and the legs acquire their bulging shapes. These are already stable as they are. Nonetheless, the pressure is increased a little further, which gives the legs a wrinkled visual appearance. Although this is not necessary from a statics viewpoint, it is a design feature that visualises the forming process. In our view, the appeal of this piece of furniture lies in this legibility of the production method, combined with a material that one does not associate with inflation. In addition, in the case of the

35|1 **'Chippensteel'** chair

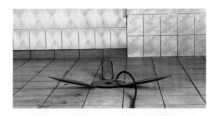

35|2 **Inflation process** of the 'Plopp' stool

37|1 First inflatable steel beam
as rolled goods, produced in a
limited edition as a design object

36|1 FiDU team at work

37|2 List of all **elements of the SxM pavilion**

38|1 The **FiDU football**, consisting of 90 parts, was presented to coincide with Euro 2008.

38|2 'Plopp' stool subject to **load testing**. With a load-bearing capacity of 2.5 tonnes, use requirements are exceeded.

'Plopp' stool it is easy to see how it has been produced. Anyone who has ever inflated a floating tire will be familiar with the process. It may be so that, in an increasingly complex world in which we are surrounded by so many things the manufacture of which we don't understand, we simply find such an object sympathetic: an authentic, coherent design that is one hundred percent true to the material – and yet, with an appearance not usually associated with the material used.

DIN 8550 defines the buckling and crumpling of sheet metal as something that is erroneous. Not being mechanical engineers, and in complete ignorance of this standard, we discovered the potential of these 'defects' as a method of stabilisation and a new formal language – even intensive and deliberate mistake-making can sometimes lead to success. The opportunity arose to present the 'Plopp' to the public at the 'Salone Internazionale del Mobile' 2007 in Milan. Here, the stool was placed on a pedestal at the world's biggest furniture fair, surrounded by numerous sheet metal exhibits intended to describe its development, concealing its interior behind a baby-blue paint coating, somewhat reminiscent of a typical former East German Trabant car. The visitors' faces expressed astonishment as they touched the 'plastic stool' in passing, unable to reconcile its haptic and visual effect. An amazing effect – the colour and formal language associated with softness and plasticity combined with the haptic feedback of metal attracted a degree of attention that exceeded all expectations and led us to actually wanting to produce the 'Plopp'. Since nobody was prepared to manufacture a piece of furniture using such a strange production method, this ultimately led to Oskar Zieta now working not just as a research fellow at the ETH, but also as a producer and entrepreneur in his native Poland. This puts him in the comfortable position of equally emphasising all three areas of production, research, and development, with each benefiting from shared expertise. The production facility in Zielona Gora now employs 15 employees and comprises equipment and personnel to manufacture FiDU elements professionally and economically, also in large quantities. The development work in Zurich is supported by an office in Wroclaw, which also organises distribution. And for all new and future projects, the research institute at the ETH Zurich offers prominent support and ensures interdisciplinary networking from mechanical engineering to material research.

Inspiration from nature

In nature, nothing is wasted. It is essential for the future that we adopt this as a model and use material and energy effectively. All processes in nature take place with a minimal use of materials and at low temperatures. Nonetheless, this results in incomparably stable and efficient structures, the forms of which appeal to our aesthetic sense. If one considers its content, stability, and use of materials, an egg is probably still the best packaging in the world. Calcite structures of algae, optimised for maximum stability combined with low weight, resemble works of sacred architecture. In a sense, perhaps we instinctively recognise good, efficient designs and find these 'beautiful' (39|1). The study of these interrelations is still at a very early stage, but possibly the appeal of FiDU products indicates an intriguing intersection between natural aesthetics and the aesthetics of artificial forms.

One possible explanation lies in the constant that all matter strives to attain the most disorganised state possible and the lowest level of energy possible. Thus, a chain hangs slack between two points and, under the influence of gravity, assumes a low energy level. If this form is inverted, an ideal form for dispersing opposing forces is created. This is how Antoni Gaudí optimised the statics of his 'Sagrada Família' in Barcelona (39|2). In metal forming with FiDU, we do not compress and stretch the material; the deformation occurs where the material can most readily yield. Without a die or forming tool, a form is produced that behaves in an astonishingly stable manner when bearing loads. Here as well, we are only just beginning to understand the particular interrelations.

However, even today we know enough to design FiDU objects according to a formal language that is inspired by nature. Planning enlarged cross-sections at points where stability is required and reduced cross-sections at the point where minor stress is applied to the structure comprises a procedure that is derived from the FiDU method. Surprisingly, this often corresponds very well with the rules of the FiDU alphabet. As result, the 'standard' actually has to be redefined in view of FiDU. Since we are not tied to semi-finished products such as tubes and beams, with FiDU a standard product is only limited by the sheet metal formats – and sheet metal is available as coils of 0.8 millimetres in thickness and up to 4 km in length. This way, several points in space can be connected without any problem by means of a single element with varying cross sections. The trade fair stand created in 2010 for Architonic illustrates this potential.

In FiDU elements, cross section changes do not play any role in terms of the process, which means that forms that reflect related properties can easily be produced. In analogy to bones, not only does this give rise to a formal language inspired by biology, this also offers the possibility of saving material and construction where these are not necessary.

39|1 Coccolithophorid algae as an example of a bionic structure that appeals to our aesthetic sense

39|2 Inverted hanging **chain model** of Antoni Gaudí's 'Sagrada Família' church in Barcelona

The two-dimensional potential

Essentially, the process of inflation is very simple. It requires nothing more than an expanding medium – usually water or air, but experiments are currently being carried out with expansive foams. Because the process is so simple, it can be situated at the site of use, the advantage of which is that the elements can be transported flat. For example, a 3 x 4 metre large structure was to be created for an exhibition in Copenhagen (41|2). Since inflation took place on site, it was – very much to the amazement of the exhibition organisers – possible to stow this without any problem in a camper van together with four passengers.

For the London Design Festival in the courtyard of the Victoria and Albert Museum, even larger elements were successfully realised (40|1). Due to difficulties with access, the 30 metre long arches were rolled up for transport and unrolled automatically through the inflation process. This size clearly transcends the architecturally relevant scale, but offers interesting ideas for large structures, such as wind power installations (41|1) and masts for above-ground transmission lines. We can see a potential in situations where transport is problematic and the work carried out at the site of use needs to be kept as simple as possible – whether in the field of space travel or in the mining industry.

The 'hollow' potential

Due to the production process, FiDU elements are hollow bodies; however, the internal pressure is released following deformation. This leads to another exciting possibility for these elements: adaptive load-bearing structures. Large elements can already be formed by applying low pressure of less than half a bar. If the pressure is maintained following deformation, for instance 0.5 bar means that buckling is resisted by a force of 5 tonnes per square metre. There are related technologies such as Tensairity, which uses airbeams under low internal pressure to create stable load-bearing structures. The load-bearing capacity of FiDU elements can be almost doubled by applying pressure. This makes it possible to react to loads, to optimise systems in terms of usability, and to counteract extreme events by increasing pressure. Another possible application is in electric vehicles in which, due to the low capacity and high weight of the batteries, the overall weight represents a decisive factor. In this case, the structure could be designed for normal operation and in the event of a crash could quickly be made rigid, in a similar way to an airbag, by means of a gas generator. A similar application involves crash barriers made of FiDU elements, which we have patented. The thin-walled hollow FiDU elements are already extremely effective as such, and help save material, which in the case of a crash barrier isn't even actually required most of the time. Only when someone hits the barrier, its bracing and energy-dissipating function is required. The thin metal sheets display a good response behaviour and a high initial deformability, and thus, ensure an efficient dissipation of energy. Rigidity can be reinforced in a targeted way by increasing the internal pressure by means of gas generators, similar to an airbag, and brace a vehicle's impact. The triggering of a gas generator could, in addition, be linked to sensors and used to detect the locations of accidents and transmit this information to a control centre.

40|1 30 metre long **inflatable steel beams** produced for an installation at the Victoria and Albert Museum in London. Their width was determined by the width of the museum's doors. They were erected by injecting compressed air, which caused the elements to unroll and unfold.

Material, Information, Technology – Options for the Future

Thus, FiDU elements offer numerous new and exciting possibilities for structural applications. That they have thus far been used most widely in the field of design is, of course, attributable to the convenient size of a piece of furniture in comparison to a facade. The advantage is that every aspect has to be solved on a small scale – production steps, working methods, and structural design. The results can then be scaled up as required. Many of the FiDU rules that have since been established still await their future large-scale implementation.

41|1 **Low-cost wind turbine** made of FiDU elements forming a vertical-axis rotor with aerodynamic profile. The elements are lighter, more stable, and significantly cheaper than conventional blades.

41|2 **'SeaHorse'** assembled from FiDU elements

Parametric Design Systems – a Current Assessment from the Designer's Viewpoint

Text   Nils Fischer

Blob-architecture, non-standard-architecture, or free-form architecture refers to structures and designs that possess complex, flowing, often rounded and biomorphic forms, which are based on free-form curves (splines), and which only become conceivable for architects through modern design software. One of the pioneers of blob architecture was the American architect Greg Lynn.

cf: Hauschild, Moritz; Karzel, Rüdiger: Digital Processes. Munich 2010, p. 105

Where do we stand now, nearly two decades after the visitation of Lynn's blob? Actually, just where we always were. Because in principle and since time immemorial, each generation of architects has sought its own reference framework. Designers have always endeavoured to place their work in a systematic context, and by doing so, advance something , create new relationships with society and the environment, produce relevance. Conversely, the differentiation between architecture and fine art was always based on the need to fulfil rather mundane criteria, such as usability, feasibility, and stability, yet also to be able to illustrate and demonstrate these criteria systematically – or to sell the product.

Seen in these terms, systematised design doesn't comprise anything novel, but rather something fundamental. It is continually redefined and reinterpreted, similarly as architecture itself. However – and this is certainly worth writing about – each generation of architects encounters a wide range of influences on the systematisation of the design process: for my generation, the key development in this search for reference was, and is, the widespread availability of computers and the new possibilities they have created. In the past 15 to 20 years this has led to far-reaching changes not only within the illustration and production process, but also the design process.

Concerning further aspects of the integration of planning, building, and manufacturing processes, see also The Operationality of Data and Material » *p. 9*, *Industrialisation versus Individualisation* » *p. 21, 25*, *Material, Information, Technology* » *p. 31*, *Construction Processes of the Future* » *p. 126*

The status quo

Nowadays, with the aid of the computer, not only can we generate and visualise forms that would have been difficult to conceive and describe not too long ago. As architects, we can now describe and rationalise increasingly complex forms and geometries and illustrate these in both structural and economic terms, even when subject to the typical time and cost constraints associated with the building process.

Parametric design is a buzzword frequently used in this context. It comprises the promise of a completely interlinked planning process. Formulating fixed planning decisions followed by sequential strata of refinements within a linear process is being replaced by the dynamic notation of decision-making processes and criteria within a bidirectional computer model (45|5) – ideally, from the concept stage to completion – with the intention of completely parallelising the planning process and giving the designer the complete freedom to manipulate the design to the last moment before construction work begins.

Concerning the scope of tendencies towards individualisation, see » *p. 52 as well as The Operationality of Data and Material* » *p. 15*, *Industrialisation versus Individualisation* » *p. 24*, *Construction Processes of the Future* » *p. 128*

The discontented designer and the promise of total flexibility

This promise constitutes an advantage for designers who continually seek an ever better solution. In fact, there is a strong correlation between the number of iterations of a design theme and the quality of the result. However, we are still far from fulfilling this promise; the complete integration of the planning process within a homogeneous system remains an often postulated, but as yet unmet goal. It involves not only software environments and interfaces with specialist planners and manufacturers, but also aspects such as limitations of liability, demarcating disciplinary responsibilities, and legal aspects of tendering processes. This is where the parallelisation of the planning process, which in ideal terms means that working drawings are integrated in the preliminary design, encounters legal and competition-based limits.

43|1 Station of the Nordkettenbahn, Innsbruck (A) 2007, Zaha Hadid Architects

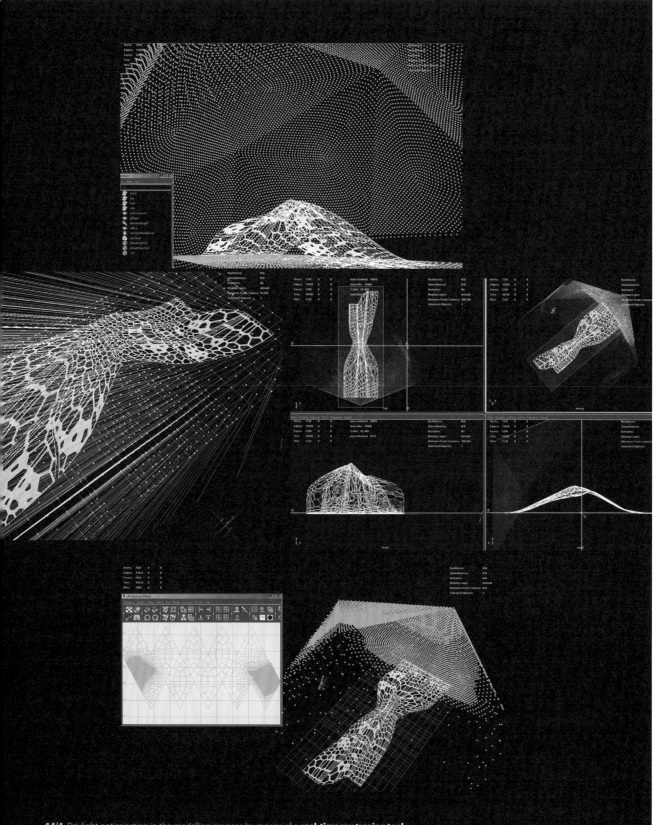

Daylight optimisation in the modelling process by means of a **real-time ray tracing tool**

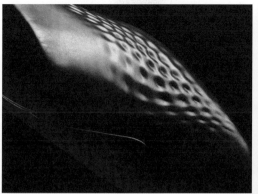

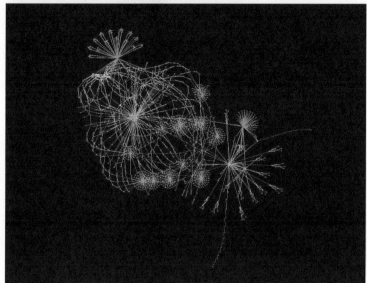

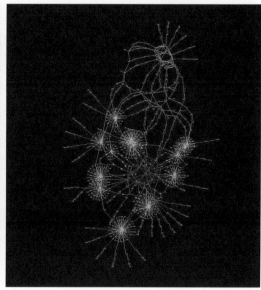

45|1 The formal principles of parametric design are independent of scale. **Zaha Hadid Footwear for Lacoste**, 2009

45|2 Ornamented surface, **Cairo Stone Towers** (ET)

45|3 and 45|4 **Node graphs** as abstract logic models are complex and develop their own aesthetic dimension.

45|5 **Bidirectional model** of the design process

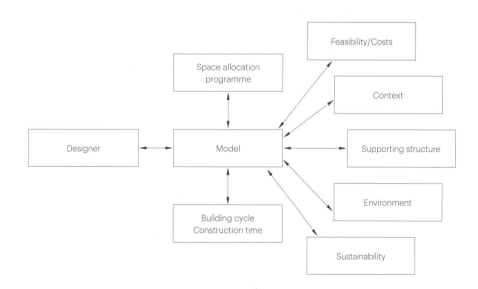

Influence on the design

46|1 Interior, **Guangzhou Opera House**, Guangzhou (CN) 2010, Zaha Hadid Architects

An object is described as self-similar *if a part of the object has the same or a similar structure as the original object following enlargement. Examples include the Sierpinski triangle or romanesco.*

cf: http://www.natur-struktur.ch/fraktale/selbstaehnlich.html (accessed on 18.11.2011)

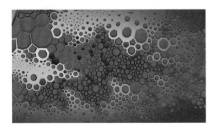

46|2 **Real-time design** of complex surfaces

However, parametric design systems provide designers with a powerful tool, which in the past two decades initially led to an explosion of experiments situated someplace between art and architecture. These influenced a whole generation of students and had a lasting effect on the current architectural language.

The possibility of linking together a wide range of information or parameters, weaving complex networks of information, and illustrating these geometrically has led to a detachment from the spatial and abstract principles of Modernism. In place of geometrical basic forms and joining principles, we now find typologies that can be mixed and moulded or arranged and merged together in broader contexts according to mathematical and natural principles. The rediscovery of the ornament – albeit in a self-similar, rather than a symmetrical form – is more and more spreading from the avantgarde into the mainstream, in addition to an interweaving and contextualisation of architecture. This coincides with the progressing development of the interface between design and production, as well as the resulting increase in cost efficiency and the improved capacity of displaying economic characteristics.

However, this dissociation from a formal canon that can be clearly geometrically defined extends beyond the formal experiment, due to its current broad availability. This means that sheer complexity or free-form geometry currently no longer represents an independent quality criterion – neither as aesthetic justification nor as communicative 'novelty factor'. Architecture needs to be able to deliver more: following an undoubtedly important period of experimentation, standards of design-based relevance are also applied to computer-generated architecture. A conscious engagement with the design object and a reorientation from the formal experiment to the 'why' behind each design was and still is the key to good architecture. Here, the quality and efficiency of the interaction with the design model plays an important role.

From the abstract expert system to 'digital modelling clay'

From the viewpoint of the designer, one interesting tendency in recent years is that the computer as a tool for creating forms is undergoing a transformation from a misappropriated expert system into an intuitive construction kit. Parametric design software is becoming increasingly accessible for direct visual interaction, not least due to better software interfaces, specific developments for architects, and a dramatic increase in affordable computing power. Whereas digital design methods were once higher alchemy for the illuminated ones with advanced programming skills and scarcely to be surpassed in terms of abstraction of the interaction with the design object, they are now part of the standard repertoire of university graduates. The topic's demystification, coinciding with the broad availability of the technology on the market, is also giving rise to a more sober perception of the benefits and limitations of the methodology.

As with any new medium, in the case of parametric design limitations were explored and the depth of opportunities was traversed within experiments that were, to a certain degree, radical. Then, from the diversity of approaches and postulates, those were distilled and ordered that proved to be beneficial. A new formal language in the current avantgarde has clearly emerged from this process, albeit in the form of a transition rather than a radical break. Parallel to the systematisation of the design language, the more practicable and pragmatic approaches have distanced themselves from the dogmatic theories of the early days: what remained and has been incorporated into the canon of contemporary architecture are the rules, forms, and processes that create an aesthetic or economic added value. Or both, depending on one's point of view, in addition to the tools that, interestingly, provide the designer with an increased capacity for intuition and freedom and offer design greater relevance, instead of degrading architects to soon-to-be-redundant operators of a deterministic design machine, as had often been feared.

Real-time design environments and intuitive interaction

For the past six years the research group CODE (computational design research group) at Zaha Hadid Architects has been examining numerous parametric programs and techniques developed by the firm's designers. These were developed almost as a by-product of their work and were optimised and advanced prior to making them available to a wider group of users within the firm. The most successful and influential methods were always those that are capable of communicating with the designer visually and in real time. Interestingly, we can see a clear trend towards an environment in which powerful visualisation and calculation systems liberate the architect from the 'burden' of technical-mechanical (engineering) considerations in their interaction with the design object and enable them to concentrate more on their actual strengths – making decisions on the basis of aesthetic and functional considerations.

Good design tools give back to the architect what they increasingly seem to have lost in the course of the industrialisation of the building and planning process: direct interaction with the model, which can lead to a great increase in quality. The key to this is: real time.

The research group CODE believes that the creative potential of designers can only be fully expressed in direct and intuitive interaction with the object. Essentially, architectural design is an ongoing process of optimi-

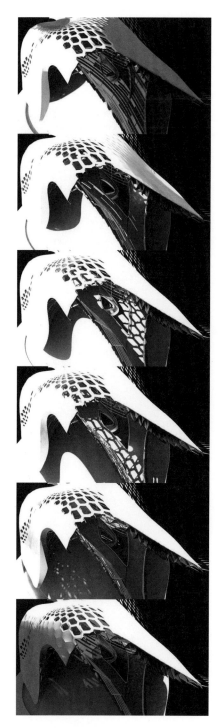

47|1 Roof studies for a low-energy pavilion, **Gui River Research Complex**, Peking (CN)

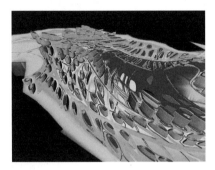

48|1 **Real-time representation of sightlines**: ray intersection as a measure for privacy on an urban scale. Appur Township, Chennai (IND)

'Intelligent clay' or 'digital clay' describes a digital modelling clay, a kind of intelligent lump of clay, which not only allows intuitive modelling and forming, but also provides equally intuitive feedback on important properties of the design.

sation, with a large number of variables that need to be continually perfected and collectively serve to establish the most satisfactory solution possible. By far, the human brain is the most powerful tool available to us for such processes of continuous consideration and iterative reappraisal of a wide range of different solutions. The aim of the research group's work is to create a design environment that, with the most effective possible use of the most recent calculation and simulation processes, places the fewest possible layers of abstraction between designer and object – a design environment that we can refer to figuratively as 'intelligent clay', an interface that allows the designer to work as intuitively as possible, while important decision-making parameters are communicated in real time.

Here, the visual perception channel assumes a key function. As of this moment, we have arrived at an interesting point with parametric design models where the technology required for visualisation is inexpensive enough, indeed almost universally available.

Why is this so important? To return to the original thesis: there is a fundamental relationship between the number of possible iterations of a design theme and the quality of a design. The faster the interaction, the greater the number of possible iterations per unit of time. And time is an increasingly limiting factor, as the following explanation shows.

How much time is available for designing?

Let us consider an exemplary and somewhat simplified timescale for the design of e.g. a large cultural building authored by an international practice actively participating in competitions:

One may think of construction projects as protracted affairs, and particularly in the case of large projects, it seems that plenty of time should be available for thorough deliberation within the creative process. However, looking at how much time remains in practice for form-finding, the quick realisation can be made that enormous time pressure exists at the 'front end' of the process.

Let us assume that such a project will last five years, with approximately 36 months dedicated to construction. With traditional tendering procedures, about 24 months for planning remain. And, at the end of this period, the architect must know very precisely what the building is going to look like. The design should be completed, and in addition, working drawings and tendering packages finished.

And how much of the approximately 24 months planning time remains for the development of the design? Well, the aforementioned working drawings and tendering process lasts pretty much a whole year. However, before work can even be started on the detail planning, the architect needs – a design.

The remaining year still sounds like plenty of time; enough to come up with a good idea. But: during the course of this year a building permit must be obtained, depending on country or region a wide range of different safety checks must be conducted, and various cost targets need to be achieved. This phase, referred to in English as 'detailed proposals' and in a rather misleading way in German as 'design' also takes 6 to 8 months. And here as well, something should already be available at the beginning, something that architects and specialist planners can refer to as they embark on this costly process – a robust design.

Of course, this needs to be signed off beforehand by the client in the form of a preliminary design with corresponding programme and budgeting. This preliminary design phase, referred to in English as the 'schematic design', will most likely take up to 3 to 4 months. And at the beginning of this phase, it is necessary to win the competition or client – you guessed it – with a design.

In practice, the competition participant ultimately only has 3 to 6 weeks left to produce this design.

But wait – there's more: these 3 to 6 weeks are, by no means, a linear timeframe allowing the design team to sit back, relax, and reflect on architecture. In the first one or two weeks, the topic and the site are inspected, research undertaken, design parameters formulated in the classic sense, and design goals defined. And in the final two or three weeks every possible resource is devoted to producing, developing, printing, filing, polishing, packing up, and shipping. Therefore, only a few weeks remain in which the actual design is created. Or, rather, the promise of a design.

Relevance of the design sketch

The problem with using modern computer systems or, strictly speaking, the second phase of digitisation of the architectural practice, which precedes parametric design, is identified within the phase of creating the design and illustrating it. This phase began with the replacement of the drawing board by the digitiser, then proceeding to the wider discovery of the computer as a visualisation tool. The problem: a sketch is now no longer a sketch.

Anyone who nowadays wishes to win a major competition not only has to submit 8 to 10 high-resolution renderings in ready-for-publication quality. Participants may even be necessitated to provide five minutes of film in HD with subtitles in Mandarin, plus cost estimate and construction timetable.

One may think that a specialist jury would be familiar with the circumstances of creating a presentation and be able to properly assess the quality of work as well as the possible breadth of interpretation it may offer. Unfortunately, however, such knowledge is not typically passed on

49|1 Competition, design of the surface and construction phase, **Heydar Aliyev Cultural Centre**, Baku (AZ) 2007–present, Zaha Hadid Architects

to the awarding authority, which in the case of public construction projects is often represented by large committees with a changing line-up of members. These often regard the submitted material as an exact representation of the finished building – and the architect then spends the next 4.75 years under the expectation of delivering the promised design, pixel for pixel, within the stipulated cost framework and time schedule. Of course, this isn't just the fault of the awarding authority. Architects have always considered the convincing representation of their ideas as a competitive advantage and have always striven for realism in their illustration. However, at this point in time expectations as to the precise predictability of the implementation of design ideas are enormous. And particularly for architects who like to test the limits of what is technically feasible, this means a lot of work in this early phase of the design.

Highly enriched real-time environments

Aside from a convincing idea and powerful images, a successful design, whether for a competition or a direct sales pitch, also requires an in-depth documentation on the feasibility of the project within the stipulated time and cost framework. The basic rule is: the less conventional your design, the more questions are asked. In fact, you are much more likely to find sceptics on a design jury than passionate advocates. Typically, related questions already have to be answered before the presentation of the project. With specialist planners as our partners, we tend to incorporate more and more levels of illustration and interpretation in the presentation of a design already at an early stage, in order to ensure an idea's capacity for survival through what could be called a pre-emptive reaction to objections: structural concepts that indicate distribution of forces, rationalisation studies for facades – an absolute must particularly in the case of curved surfaces – the analysis of environmental influences such as thermal intake, wind and weather, energy flow simulations, traffic flow, cost planning, in major projects even construction timetable planning etc. These are increasingly the subject of complex simulations at the earliest phase, which influence the design in its genesis and increase its relevance and robustness in relation to critical questions.

We identify a change from a linear process of information enrichment, beginning with a simple sketch, which is successively saturated by additional layers of technical and organisational considerations in the course of a project, towards a multilayered technical analysis at the earliest design stage. Its fuzziness is adapted to the demanded speed of iteration and successively reduced (50|1) – similar to a bubbling primordial soup that contains all information and possibilities, yet reveals increasingly clear outlines and more precise differentiations as it cools.

Parametric design provides the opportunities for this: live interfaces

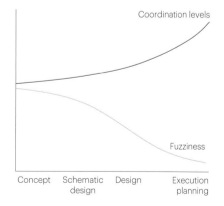

Coordination levels

Fuzziness

Concept Schematic   Design   Execution
         design   planning

50|1 Progress of the **parametric, bidirectional design process**

between expert systems make it possible to exchange more and more data with increasing speed and simultaneously make this data available to the designer, in order to influence the decision-making process continuously and on a variety of different levels. To make practical use of this information, the designer must be able to access it intuitively and in real time. Only in this way can the designer gain an overview of the options and gradual distinctions between solutions without being impeded in the process of design or drowning in the flood of data.

Return to the intuitive

Therefore, the focus of current developments is on systems that address the quality of interaction with the user. Fluid interaction, that is to say a low system latency, becomes a constant. The depth or precision of calculations and analyses is adapted to the computing power available in order to simultaneously provide the designer with as much relevant information as possible in direct interaction with the design object. The aim is to improve the quality of the myriads of small decisions that are made, consciously or unconsciously, during the course of creating a design.

An example: imagine a lump of clay ('intelligent clay') that changes its colour while it is being modelled. Imagine that is is, for instance, related to its complexity, i.e. essentially the manufacturing costs of its surface. Imagine that it provides feedback on the evenness of the distribution of forces through its plasticity or its temperature. Such a tool opens up the possibility of working freely, similar to a sculptor, but at the same time ensuring that highly complex parameters are fulfilled in an intuitive way, that is to say on a low level of abstraction that our brain can process quickly and instinctively. Such technologies would permit us to create a design more or less intuitively; a design that doesn't just arise from aesthetic considerations, but also implicitly meets basic architectural requirements in terms of usability and feasibility, and thus allows the designer more room for experimentation. This is the goal.

Creator versus machine?

Over the past few decades there has been much discussion concerning the influence of the computer on the quality of design and the creative act of designing – as something that opens up possibilities or as the spectre of the deterministic design machine, which automatically creates the perfect design as long as it is fed with the correct information and sufficient processing power is available. Or as the unstoppable Über-System, which continually adds to its knowledge and improves itself through genetic algorithms, and which will come to replace humans with their limited capabilities – shades of Kurzweil's singularity.

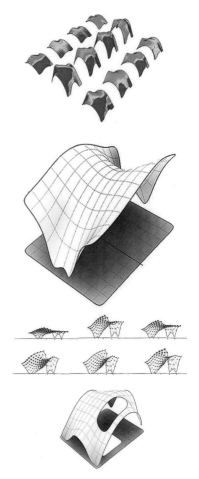

51|1 Digital form finding with irregular networks incorporating further geometric and physical parameters such as masses, internal loads, shading, etc. Gui River Research Complex, Peking (CN)

The singularity, as defined by Ray Kurzweil, is the point at which artificial systems can improve or develop further without human intervention, and technological evolution becomes completely detached from biological evolution. Already at this point in time, we use largely automated processes/software in order to develop the next generation of optimised semiconductors. In return, these permit the design of even more efficient hardware based on their increased performance.

However, the creative impulse, the aesthetic and spiritual dimension of building, and the subjective perspective of the designer, including his imperfections, always remain fundamental aspects of architecture. Here, so many small and large parameters need to be evaluated and assembled into a unique constellation. And, for a long time to come, the human brain will remain, by far, the most efficient tool for developing hypotheses that address problems with an infinite number of solutions. The computer cannot replace its ability to compensate lacking precision, its conviction in decision-making, and its use of gut instinct to navigate through unknown parts of equations. And the more effectively and directly this tool, the 'brain', can be engaged in the working process, the better and more rapidly can the hypothesis be developed that is constituted by the design. Of course, the intelligent lump of clay still remains wishful thinking, but we are moving steadily in the direction of highly interactive and highly enriched development environments for designs. Not only can these maintain the relevance of sketches in meeting the increased expectations of the market in terms of the precise implementability of a realistically visualised design sketch. They also add numerous new elements, such as structures analogous to natural phenomena and dynamic growth processes to the available repertoire of forms of expression – typologies that our perceptive apparatus can grasp intuitively, but that have become describable and calculable only in recent years.

Material efficiency and energy balance

In addition to their appealing aesthetic dimension, these typologies also possess another interesting property: in most cases, they are extremely efficient. The optimisation potential of designs in the early stage is immense. Coarse, but rapid feedback to the designer can help enable taking the efficiency of a design – in terms of energy or structure – into consideration directly and intuitively in the design process. Such approaches are by no means new, but they are usually very expensive to implement. Parametric design tools can now, for example, represent force-flow analyses and distributions of density within materials, due to the increasing availability of affordable computing power. In addition, they can make such deliberations possible in situations where time or resources for the optimisation of materials is typically absent.

Why a wider availability of such design tools can make an important contribution to the energy debate is made clear by the intensity of energy consumption within the building industry. In 2009 approximately 2.8 billion tonnes of CO_2 were released worldwide through the manufacture of cement, the most important ingredient in concrete. To put this figure into perspective: this is equivalent to roughly four times the CO_2 burden caused by global air travel. We may also consider that global steel

Concerning the scope of tendencies towards individualisation, see » *p. 43 as well as The Operationality of Data and Material* » *p. 15, Industrialisation versus Individualisation* » *p. 24, Construction Processes of the Future* » *p. 128*

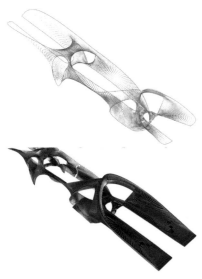

52|1 Experimental form finding supported by relaxation algorithms: each manipulation leads to a readjustment of the surface with uniform distribution of stress.

Concerning questions on energy and use of resources, see Sustainable Urban Development » *p. 72, 77, Understanding Buildings as Systems* » *p. 82–93, Common Sense instead of High-Tech* » *p. 94, Construction Processes of the Future* » *p. 125, Cooperation between Industry and Research* » *p. 130, The Research Initiative 'Future Building'* » *p. 136, 139 ff.*

53|1 **Glasgow Museum of Transport,** Glasgow (GB) 2011, Zaha Hadid Architects

production is responsible for roughly the same volume of emissions, while houses comprise some of the biggest energy consumers as well. If we project these tendencies into the future then it quickly becomes clear where the actual challenge lies: building efficiently, above all in regions where growth is taking place.

Whereas in the highly-developed industrial countries technologies for optimising designs and materials are relatively readily available and affordable within the cost framework of a construction project, in rapidly growing emerging economies and rising industrialised nations, such as China or India, planning is comparatively uniform. Even on larger scales, it is conducted in a simplified manner, not least because planning fees in these countries are far below the level of those in industrialised countries – in India, for example, even in commercial construction projects, these are often below one percent, at building costs that are low to begin with. Considering the enormous growth potential and the accelerating tendency towards urbanisation in these ascending, and for the most part, still agricultural economies (in India, 70 percent of the population live in rural areas, in China – already at this point in time the by far biggest producer and consumer of cement – the figure exceeds 50 percent) it becomes clear that more efficient planning must start here: in the emerging economies and rising industrialised nations, and on a broad basis.

One laptop per child – one architect per neighbourhood?

Interestingly, it is now possible to install practically all the tools necessary for a building project that isn't all too complex, that is well-optimised in terms of energy, and is efficient in the use of materials on a laptop similar to the one used to write this article. The key lies in the communication capacity and usability of tools, which makes it possible for planners to develop material- and energy-efficient solutions without a staff of specialist consultants, and without involving time- and cost-intensive processes. This isn't a question of replacing the architect or engineer with a software programme. Rather, the idea is to make technical and scientific know-how readily accessible in situations in which it cannot at present be made available due to cost considerations. Yet, given the sheer scale of some projects, this can provide an enormous leverage effect: in the low-end area of building technology, where simple, often manual solutions can be made more material-efficient through intelligent planning, and where a solution at perhaps only an 80 percent level of optimisation, yet considered feasible already represents an enormous improvement of the status quo.

I would like to end this perhaps somewhat wild ride though the topic with a look forward: during the past year, our firm's in-house research group held workshops at various universities in India and China over a

Concerning perspectives on urbanity and urban development, see Return to the Social » p. 66, Sustainable Urban Development » p. 71

The aim of the initiative One laptop per child *is to combat poverty in the third world with the aid of educational computers. The concept follows the philosophy of 'helping people to help themselves' and assumes that the economic development of a region can be achieved most sustainably by providing the population with education. In order to achieve the goal of sustainable public education in regions in which the infrastructure is hardly developed and children are forced to work at a very early age, a concept was developed that attempts to provide an adequate basic education within the first school years.*

According to: http://www.olpc-deutschland.de (accessed on 18.11.2011)

period of ten days and nights. At these occasions, and with the support of software developers, students were familiarised with programs and programming techniques for creating forms that also take into consideration load-bearing behaviour (55|1 and 55|3). The aim was not just to learn the technology, but to apply it. Towards the end of the workshops, the intention was for students to build a functioning version of the design in collaboration with experts in local building technologies – using bare hands and whatever materials 100 dollars could by on site. This year, for the first time and following initial experiments with light-weight planar structures based on steel mesh and with the aid of a real time FEM solver as part of the design environment, we produced light-weight free-form concrete shells with span widths of up to 10 metres in Bangalore in India. This topic was pursued in greater depth during a workshop at the Tecnologico de Monterey in Mexico City (55|2). _____

55|1 Workshop in Changsha (CN) 2010

55|2 Workshop in Mexiko City (MEX) 2011

55|3 Workshop in Bangalore (IND) 2010

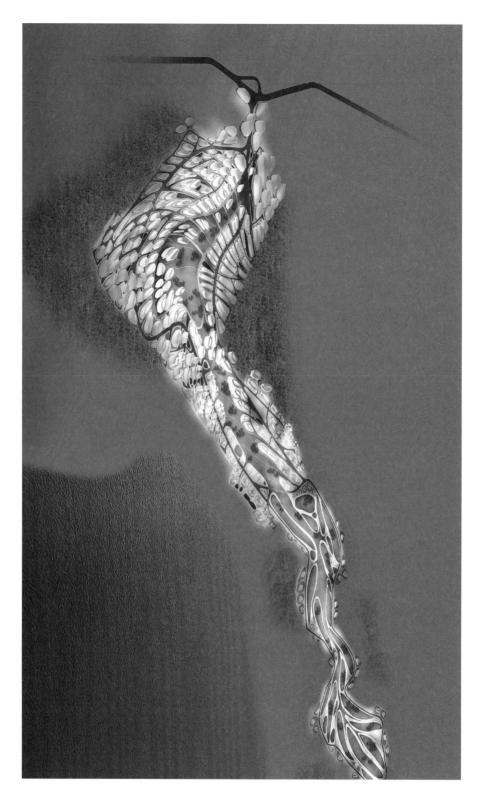

56|1 **Parametrically generated master plan** for Appur Township, Chennai (IND), Zaha Hadid Architects
57|1 **Urban Metro Cable**, Caracas (YV) 2010, Urban Think Tank

Return to Social Concerns – New Perspectives in Contemporary Architecture

Text Andres Lepik

The Prada Flagship Store in SoHo designed by Rem Koolhaas in 2001 marked a highlight in the contemporary alliance of star architects and fashion labels. The renovation of approximately 2100 square metres of retail space supposedly cost about 40 million dollars – an incredible sum even for New York, considering how much architecture was eventually visibly perceivable. Starting in the 1990s increasingly concerted efforts to arouse media attention with big names in architecture have been made by fashion labels and cultural institutions, property developers and politicians. It seemed as though the Bilbao effect, since 1994 symbolic of the economic revival of an industrial city that declined into insignificance by means of 'wow-factor' architecture, was to take place everywhere. Institutions or even entire cities aimed at gaining greater public prestige combined with additional economic success by churning out new architectural icons. This strategy was also adopted by many emerging economies such as China and the Arab Emirates – often in conjunction with a readiness to abandon valuable indigenous traditions.

Change of perspective

The economic crisis that developed in the aftermath of the collapse of the speculative real estate market in the USA in autumn 2008 and that impacted many other countries almost akin to a wildfire resulted in a change in the public perception of so-called star architecture. The pavilion designed by Zaha Hadid for Chanel in Central Park – an advertising campaign for the fashion label disguised as an art project – elicited an unmistakeably clear reaction by the critic Nicolai Ouroussoff: "The wild, delirious ride that architecture has been on for the last decade looks as if it's finally coming to an end. And after a visit to the Chanel Pavilion that opened Monday in Central Park, you may think it hasn't come soon enough."[1] This had such a profound effect that the journey of the pavilion, which had already visited Hong Kong and Tokyo, came abruptly to an end – without any protest. Escalating worries about the future of a country that was confronted with a massive rise in unemployment and poverty rates almost immediately following the crisis disclosed the luxury excesses of architecture to the general public as something that had long been propagated by some critics: empty formulas of representation without social, economic, and ecological sustainability. At the beginning of the 21st century it became clear that architecture, as the central discipline for designing humanity's spaces to work and live in was in danger of losing its social relevance. Yet, looking back to the beginning of the 20th century, intentions were quite different: the prominent representatives of modern architecture claimed that they would create a better designed world for all social classes – the theme of the second CIAM congress held in 1929 in Frankfurt am Main was the 'Minimum Subsistence Dwelling'. However, the current big stars of world architecture merely appear to be in a state of permanent competition for lucrative projects awarded by a small, yet financially potent group of clients.

The Architecture Biennale in Venice is one of the most important intellectual market places for international trends and ideas. While the motto for 2010 was 'People meet in architecture', the exhibition curated by Kazuyo Sejima was predominantly concerned with aesthetic issues, without any reference to the increasing importance of global problems such as migration, poverty, or population increase. Yet, the decision to award the Golden Lion for Best National Participation to the pavilion of the Kingdom of Bahrain set an important signal. Three huts built by fishermen using driftwood (59|1) as a place for communication and events were exemplary in their compliance with the general topic of the Biennale, while also pointing out a small, but important social problem: the sprawling real estate development on the island of Bahrain has expelled the fishermen from their traditional territories along the coast. The huts are a symbol of the simplicity and modesty of their needs, which are in stark contrast to the real estate development that threatens their exist-

1

Ouroussoff, Nicolai: Art and Commerce Canoodling in Central Park. In: New York Times, 20.10.2008

CIAM (Congrès Internationaux d'Architecture Moderne) *After the success of the Weißenhof Exhibition in Stuttgart (1927), Hélène de Mandrot, Sigfried Giedion, and Le Corbusier initiated an association of internationally renowned architects. The objective was to develop contemporary solutions to current problems of modern architecture by an annual exchange of ideas. Topics such as new possibilities of urban architecture were discussed and formulated in manifestos, including the Athens Charter (1933).*

cf: Pevsner, Nikolaus; Honour, Hugh; Fleming, John: 'Lexikon der Weltarchitektur.' [Lexicon of World Architecture.]. Munich 1999

59|1 Pavilion of the Kingdom of Bahrain, Architecture Biennale Venice (I) 2010, Bahrain Urban Research Team, LAPA-EPFL Lausanne, Camille Zakharia, Mohammed Rashid Bu Ali

For further aspects of social and societal change cf. » p. 68 as well as Sustainable Urban Development » p. 71f., Trend Predictions » p. 102, Living Ergonomics » p. 123, Research Initiative 'Future Building' » p. 137

ence, and hence also a part of the cultural identity of the country. The fact that the project was developed by a joint Swiss-Bahraini team shows that international communication has resulted in the beginning of an awareness of the social ramifications of architecture also in the Persian Gulf. The political developments in the Arabian island state since spring 2011 clearly show that the problems of the fishermen are only the tip of an iceberg of social grievances the country is confronted with.

Architecture as a social catalyst

Some architects have long been active in the effort to influence social change in a positive way through exemplary projects – especially with regard to under-supplied social strata in their own respective countries. They are not in the media limelight as of yet, but the growing number of international architectural prizes that also honour social sustainability, as well as the increasing attention such projects receive from the expert media, show that the parameters of public assessment are changing. One of these architects is Michael Maltzan from Los Angeles, who has been actively involved in solving problems in Skid Row since 1993, a neighbourhood in Los Angeles with one of the largest homeless populations in the United States since the 1930s. Commissioned by the Skid Row Housing Trust, Maltzan developed housing projects in which the homeless can gradually get used to living in a community again by means of shared spaces such as kitchens, meeting rooms, and courtyards. Maltzan's second project is Carver Apartments, which opened in 2010 and is occupied by 97 formerly homeless, mainly elderly and disabled residents (60|1 and 60|2). Residents are offered individual shelter and support as well as a common identity through a building that provides high quality of design despite a low budget. The project succeeds in transforming all of the disadvantage of the difficult location alongside a multi-lane city highway and the complexity of the social task into an advantage. Although the architect was not its initiator, this particular project, as well as several others related to social issues, have resulted in the establishment of a scope of activity in the architect's office that he is committed to pursuing in the future.

The Rural Studio in Alabama is another example of approaches that aim to reinvigorate the relation between architecture and society have existed in the USA for quite some time. This particular project is an Auburn University programme initiated in 1993 with the goal of getting architecture students directly involved in improving conditions in extremely poor areas of West Alabama, where about 30 percent of the population live below the poverty line. The student teams design and build projects that have a positive influence on the entire surrounding area – from single-family homes (61|1) and community centres to sports facilities and fire stations. More than 120 projects have been realised

60|1 and 60|2 Carver Apartments, Los Angeles (USA) 2010, Michael Maltzan Architecture

since the founding of Rural Studio. In the meantime, numerous other architecture schools in the USA followed this example, with programmes such as 'Design Build Bluff' at the University of Utah, as well as in Germany ('Design.Develop.Build' at RTHW Aachen) and Austria ('BASE-habitat' at the University of Art and Design Linz). These programmes are increasingly popular with students, because of the completely new understanding of the social dimension of their later profession conveyed at an early stage of their studies, as well as a small contribution towards making a real difference with every realised project.

Existing conditions as resource

However, not only new architecture projects can serve to stimulate and improve social processes. Aside from ecological and economic advantages, change of use and redesign of existing buildings offers opportunities to promote social changes. For a number of years, within their buildings and publications, Jean-Philippe Vassal and Anne Lacaton from Paris have been working on the development of a new social perspective for architecture. Their ideas for a sensitive renewal and improvement of building stock by avoiding demolition are not new as such, yet they do appear to be radical in the context of the past few decades. They renovated an area of 7800 square metres in the Palais de Tokyo in Paris in 2001 for just about three million Euro – what a contrast to the Prada Store by Rem Koolhaas! In collaboration with Frédéric Druot, Lacaton & Vassal developed a study called 'Plus' that is based on a series of case studies and concerned with a socially sustainable restructuring of social housing in France.2 An initial implementation on a larger scale is currently taking place with the conversion of the Tour Bois le Prêtre in Paris (61|2), which involves upgrading the apartments of a typical 1960s residential tower by addition of patio rooms and balconies. The projected overall costs to be covered by the municipal housing association are considerably lower that what demolishing the building would cost, rehousing the residents, and building a new structure. This project, which was developed together with the occupants of the house within several workshops, can be considered a signal of shifting away from the earlier 'clean slate' policy of promising a better future that follows ecological, economic, and socially sustainable strategies by tearing down problematic buildings. Here, architecture serves as a catalyst for a change in policy, while the architects become the moderators of social change.

An initiative called Haushalten e.V., situated in Leipzig, adopts a similar approach: it brings together owners of old vacant buildings and young members of the creative class and start-ups looking for low-rent premises. The initiative arranges short-term commercial lease agreements between the interested parties. The tenants of the existing structures that are called 'Guard Houses' only pay for the utility costs as well as a

61|1 $20K House II, Greensboro, Alabama (USA) 2006, Rural Studio with Auburn University architecture students

For the potential of changes of use and renovations cf. » p. 62 as well as Sustainable Urban Development » p. 73, Understanding Buildings Systems » p. 84, Common Sense Instead of High Tech » p. 99, Building Processes of Tomorrow » p. 127, Research Initiative 'Future Building' » p. 137

2

Druot, Frédéric; Lacaton, Anne; Vassal, Jean-Philippe: Plus. Large Scale Housing Development. An exceptional case. Barcelona 2007

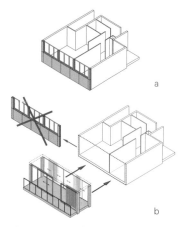

61|2 Conversion schematic, **Residential Tower Tour Bois le Prêtre**, Paris (F) 2011, Druot, Lacaton & Vassal
a Existing; b Extension

62|1 **High Line Park**, New York (USA) 2008, Diller
Scofidio + Renfro, Field Operations

*For the potential of changes of use and
renovations cf.* » *p. 61 as well as Sus-
tainable Urban Development* » *p. 73,
Understanding Buildings as Systems
» p. 84, Common Sense Instead of High
Tech* » *p. 99, Building Processes of
Tomorrow* » *p. 127, Research Initiative
'Future Building'* » *p. 137*

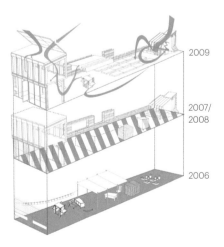

2009

2007/
2008

2006

62|2 Step-by-step conversion of the site into an
urban garden, **Passage 56**, Paris (F) 2009, atelier
d'architecture autogérée

small contribution to the initiative. The arrangement protects the houses
from decay and vandalism, while simultaneously creating new social
structures that, in some cases, have already led to long-term usage.
Moreover, the initiative's expertise is consciously employed by the City of
Leipzig in an effort to fight retail space vacancies with a comparable
model. This example illustrates how new structures can be generated by
private initiatives, which public authorities in return can effectively use
for the social and economic benefit of the entire city.

The return of the gardens

The positive economic and social effects that can be achieved by preser-
vation and intelligent change of use of existing built structures is de-
monstrated by the High Line in New York (62|1). A private initiative was
able to prevent the demolition of a 2.3 kilometres long section of a former
railroad track for freight trains running through the gallery district of
Chelsea. The track had been in disuse for many years and was transformed into a public park based on designs by architects Diller Scofido
+ Renfro and landscape planners Field Operations. Ever since the first
section was opened in June 2008 the High Line has become one of New
York's new attractions. It has improved the quality of the entire area and
lead to the construction of a number of new hotels and residential buildings in its immediate neighbourhood. This success was underscored by
the opening of a second section early in the summer of 2011. It has contributed to making the currently less developed area along the West Side
up to 30th Street more attractive. The High Line project started as a
bottom-up initiative, initially directed against the commercial interests
of real estate developers and planning policy of local government. Its
success shows that the motives of the actors involved are not necessarily
mutually exclusive.

Leftover urban spaces considered unfit for development can also be
turned into neighbourhood meeting places: this is exemplified by 'Pas-
sage 56' in Paris (62|2). A plot of land that served as a passageway was
converted into an urban garden by Constantin Petcou and Doina
Petrescu and their office atelier d'architecture autogérée (aaa) in collaboration with local residents. The garden is considered an exemplary social
and ecological project. All the energy necessary for operation is gained
from solar cells, the required water is collected from the roofs, and ferti-
liser is provided by composting toilets. An additional event space was
built within a municipal training programme for unemployed youth,
using recycled as well as inexpensive local materials. A group of residents takes care of the garden and organises events there. In line with
the principles of aaa, which define the role of the architect as initiator
and facilitator of autonomous processes, a self-organised structure was
created here that can be transferred to similar disused spaces without

any further involvement of the architects. In terms of its dimensions, the project can be considered a kind of urban acupuncture – an intervention focussed on a very small site, but with a very positive influence on the whole surrounding area. Marco Clausen and Robert Shaw, the founders of Nomadisch Grün, started a similar initiative on a larger area with the 'Princess Gardens' (Prinzessinnengärten) near the Moritzplatz in Kreuzberg, Berlin. For years and without success the city had tried to sell the site that now has been transformed into a neighbourhood garden where agricultural crops are grown and theoretical and practical knowledge in the field of gardening and horticulture is offered in courses and various events. The garden was designed as a temporary project that functions without built structures, in order to be able to hand over the rented site at short notice as soon as the city finds a suitable buyer. Targeted new cultivation of garden areas in urban environments, also on larger scales, is currently becoming increasingly popular in shrinking cities, such as Dessau or Detroit. While the initiatives of 'urban farming' on residual spaces in densely built cities do not lead to any significant level of self-supply, they rather fulfil a social purpose on a small scale. Yet, the design of actively used garden areas is a central element in a design-based redefinition of such shrinking cities.

In the favelas

According to estimations by UN-HABITAT more than one third of the world's population currently lives in slums or comparable informal settlements. Most of these are located in the southern hemisphere and rates are increasing. Approaching the subject of favelas in terms of policy and urban planning has become a central issue also among architects, and especially in Central and South America. Since the problem has become so immense, in addition to being part of an historical process, results cannot be achieved quickly.

Back in 1965, a significant effort to address the unplanned development of informal settlements through urban planning strategies was the Proyecto Experimental de Vivienda (PREVI) in Lima, Peru, initiated by the president of state at the time, Fernando Belaúnde Terry, who was a an architect. Luminaries of the international architectural avantgarde, among them James Stirling and Aldo van Eyck, were invited to participate in the project, with the support of the United Nations. They were asked to design a settlement with 1500 apartments for people with extremely low income. Each house should offer the opportunity of expansion at a later stage. Because of the military coup in 1968, building didn't begin before 1974 and only 500 houses were completed. Despite the positive results, the project wasn't repeated for a long time.

In 1993 in Brazil, the architect Jorge Mario Jauregui began initiating a step-by-step improvement of the living conditions in the shanty towns

The United Nations Centre for Human Settlements – (UNCHS/HABITAT) – was established in 1978 after the first UN Conference on Human Settlements in Vancouver and transferred to the United Nations Programme for Human Settlements (UN-HABITAT) in 2002. UN-HABITAT is the central organisation of the UN in the field of urban development, settlements, and housing in developing and emerging countries. The organisation is based in Nairobi, Kenya. It aims at supporting sustainable urban development.

cf: http://www.bmz.de (accessed on 20.10.2011)

Informal settlements *(also referred to as slum, spontaneous settlement, shanty town, squatter settlement, bairro, favela, barong-barong, bastee) developed and are still developing in large and small cities in the course of urbanisation processes. Their deficiencies are related to legal status, infra structure, and public services. While the term 'informal settlement' stresses the lack of land ownership of the residents, the term 'slum' emphasizes the inadequate infrastructural facilities of these settlements.*

cf: http://www.gtz.de/de/dokumente/de-flyer-slum-sanierung.pdf (accessed on 20.10.2011)

of Rio de Janeiro through many small measures within the Favela-Bairro project. Within the projects for the favelas Complexo do Alemão and Complexo de Manguinhos, the local government of Rio is now starting to accelerate processes of urbanisation. This includes, in particular, the linkage of its estimated 600 favelas to the formally planned city by connection to the local public transport system and the sewage system, by provision of medical care and educational institutions, etc. on a larger scale and at a faster rate: the city intends to improve its image for the Football World Cup 2014. The housing construction authority SEHAB (Secretaria Municipal de Habitação) in São Paulo also currently runs an extensive programme that is funded by very large sums of money provided by the government and involves external architects. The aim is to employ a number of measures to end the decades-long repression and marginalisation of large parts of society in a clearly visible way, and at the same time to ensure that the urban community as a whole benefits from the changes, both socially and ecologically.

Another concept was developed in Chile by the architect Alejandro Aravena and the company Elemental, founded by Aravena (in conjunction with the Universidad Católica de Santiago and the fuel company COPEC). It aims to convert social housing construction into a tool for step-by-step urbanisation and legalisation, as well as a positive investment for the urban and national economy. The project's first residential complex for 93 families realised in Iquique in the north of the country has become a great success. Only a supporting and earthquake-safe basic structure of the building is provided (66|1), while further building measures are carried out by the owners themselves (66|2). This was the only way to keep building costs down to 7500 dollars per house. The occupants can buy the houses with a loan from the municipality, and as property owners, no longer have to live with the constant fear of demolition and eviction typical of informal settlements. This results in significant changes both for the residents as well as for the city as a whole: the former exclusion is transformed into participation and economic interrelation. Since then, roughly 1000 further units have been realised by Elemental in Chile in a similar manner. Elemental is convinced that social housing construction can also be carried out profitably, and in the long run become economically beneficial for the state, the residents, and the architects.

In order to infuse the architectural profession with a renewed social dimension, architects should not wait for political change, but become active themselves. A good example for this is the project 'Urban Metro Cable' in Caracas, Venezuela. Since 1998 the architects Alfredo Brillembourg and Hubert Klumpner and their office Urban Think Tank (UTT) have dedicated themselves to finding a way to bridge the extreme social divide between the informal city and the formally planned city. Changing this situation is of extreme urgency, since the enormous crime rates in

For perspectives of urbanity and urban development cf. Parametric Design Systems » p. 54, Sustainable Urban Development » p. 71

66|1 and 66|2 Basic structure, owner-built infill structures, **social housing**, Iquique (RCH) 2005, Alejandro Aravena

Return to Social Concerns – New Perspectives in Contemporary Architecture

the megacities of Latin America are directly related to the frustration in the slums caused by the absence of adequate schools, clinics, sports facilities, police protection, and local transport systems. Of the five million inhabitants of Caracas, about one million live in the bairros. The proposal by Urban Think Tank to build an aerial cable car to connect the settlements along a steep slope to the public local transport system of the city was initially turned down by the city council, who merely intended to connect the illegal settlements to the city with streets. However, this would have resulted in a significant destruction of social networks, since hillside road building would have required tearing down about 25 percent of the existing buildings and relocating the people who live there. When the attention of the country's president, Hugo Chavez, was directed towards UTT's idea, it was declared a project of political urgency and realised by the city. The cable car has been in operation since January 2010 and offers residents a fast connection to the public transport system (64–65|1 and 67|1). This first step was followed by many more: a second cable car for another bairro in Caracas is under construction.

67|1 **Urban Metro Cable**, Caracas (YV) 2010, Urban Think Tank

A similar strategy of social pacification through architecture and infrastructure was also implemented in Medellín in Columbia. In 2004 the former mayor of the city, Sergio Fajardo, started to turn some of the districts of the city that were notorious for drug-related crime into 'normal' places to live in by building schools and cultural institutions and providing connections to local public transport. Of course, reurbanisation measures on this scale can only be successful with political pressure and government financing. However, in combination with high-quality architectural design, they offer the city dwellers new opportunities for identification. The Biblioteca España in Medellín by Giancarlo Mazzanti, opened in 2005, is an example of how a former 'no-go' area can be turned into a new public place for meeting (68|1 and 68|2).

Restart

In contemporary society, the legitimisation of architecture can no longer achieved by ever more complex acrobatics in shape and material. Architecture should instead return to dealing with basic questions of necessity and set new standards for sustainability and economy. The 'Jellyfish Theatre' in London represents an antithesis to projects such as the Chanel Pavilion by Zaha Hadid. This similarly temporary structure comprises 120 seats and was designed by the architecture and art team Folke Köbberling and Martin Kaltwasser (69|2). Built on a near-zero budget, it was driven by the active enthusiasm of unemployed architects, carpenters, and other volunteer helpers. After a construction period of only nine weeks in the summer of 2010 and by using only recycled and donated building material, such as euro pallets, it was dis-

Andres Lepik

67

68|1 and 68|2 Biblioteca España, Medellín (CO) 2005, Giancarlo Mazzanti

The Aga Khan Award for Architecture *rewards projects displaying excellence in architecture, planning, restoration, and landscape design in three-year intervals. The award is not only one of the most financially beneficial prizes in the world, it also specifies an unambiguously social requirement: the most important criterion is that the structure influences its environment in a positive way. The jury is comprised of international architects, scientists, artists, and experts involved in development-related work.*

cf: http://www.akdn.org/architecture/information asp; http://www.detail.de/artikel_aga-khan-award_27054_De.htm (accessed on 20.10.2011)

For further aspects of social and societal change cf. » p. 60 as well as Sustainable Urban Development » p. 71f., Trend Predictions » p. 102, Living Ergonomics » p. 123, Research Initiative 'Future Building' » p. 137

mantled again after being in use for six weeks, and of course, recycled. In general, a very important aspect of the ongoing new orientation of architecture is the return to local materials. A brilliant example of how a method created thousands of years in the past and that remained in use in Europe up to the early 20th Century, such as the rammed-earth technique, can be reinvented for contemporary housing construction is a house built by Martin Rauch in 2007. Located in Schlins in the Austrian Federal State of Vorarlberg, the structure uses the very material obtained from the excavation pit and combines ecological and technological experimentation with first-class aesthetic design (69|1). Here, Martin Rauch demonstrates impressively how new perspectives can be achieved by rediscovering the forgotten potentials of adobe or loam-based building methods, given that such building techniques receive increased attention in research and development. The significance of this kind of building also lies in the fact that the new appreciation of such techniques in highly developed countries also has a positive effect on developing and emerging countries, where loam-based construction is still considered a backward method. Back in the 1940s, the Egyptian architect Hassan Fahty began his efforts to counter the growing industrialisation of construction. In Egypt as well, international modernism and its materials of choice, concrete, steel and glass, emerged triumphant. Fahty emphasised a different style of construction, rooted in local traditions – alas, unsuccessfully. However, the tradition of loam-based building has received renewed attention as a reimport to developing countries. One example is Francis Kéré, who was born in Burkina Faso and studied at the TU Berlin, where he was able to gain an improved understanding of the ecological and economic issues and needs of his home country. He set an important signal in Burkina Faso with his school building in Gando. The fact that he received the Aga Kahn Award for the project led to the recognition of the prototypical quality of this work in developing countries. There are further examples, such as Anna Heringer, who developed an award-winning project in collaboration with Eike Roswag with a school built of loam and other natural materials in Bangladesh. Or Emilio Caravatti, who tries to raise the prestige of loam-based building with his own foundation in Mali. This exemplifies that the knowledge gained at architectural schools in developed countries can, indeed, be transferred to developing countries to achieve a sustainable and positive influence on the social dimension of building.

Local and global

New important approaches in contemporary architecture very often emerge when architects actively concern themselves with problematic social issues and develop related practical solutions. Precisely because such initiatives, as 'unsolicited architecture' (i.e. architecture that finds its clients and sites by itself), arise beyond the established mechanisms and dependencies between architects and their clients, this leads to a diversity of interesting approaches with potential for further development. In contrast to their historical 20th-century predecessors, these commitment-driven projects are not based on contemporary political or social theories, but usually have a more direct and practical basis. Success can only be expected to be achieved slowly, requiring a degree of personal involvement, precise knowledge of the local conditions, and inclusion of the prospective users. In an ideal case, such planning instruments are then adopted by policymakers, in order to realise a broader and sustainable effect on a larger scale. Socially committed projects are particularly radical in their rejection of the luxuriousness and celebrity cult of the past decades and in their search for solutions to questions of design that concern humanity in its entirety. This active consideration of the 'other' 90 per cent of the world population, the huge proportion of humanity that does not typically enjoy the benefit of 'architecture', is a decisive requirement for the social dimension of architecture to regain a new credibility in the eyes of the public. ———————————————

69|1 **Single-family house**, Schlins (A) 2007, Planning Team Roger Boltshauser and Martin Rauch

69|2 **Jellyfish Theatre** temporary venue, London (GB) 2010, Folke Köbberling, Martin Kaltwasser

Sustainable Urban Development in a Relational Framework

Text   Alain Thierstein, Anne Wiese, Isabell Nemeth

Far-reaching economic, social, and ecological changes over the past years have caused a fundamental alteration in the framework conditions of urban development. Some changes are universally applicable, while others are local and specific. Particularly the increasing differentiation of a hierarchy of cities and the development of a global network transcend spatial boundaries. Global material cycles give rise to ecological and economic effects in many places, while these can also be of local origin in others. In Europe, the transformation into a knowledge society is in full swing. Urban diversity has gained a new appreciation and is becoming a location factor among creative and heavily knowledge-based service providers. Global relations and local milieus are equally becoming important factors for urban development. Increasingly supra-regional fields of activity of companies favour moving particularly space-consuming activities to other locations inside or outside the country. The gaps created thereby require a reinterpretation within the framework of the city. These kinds of displacement processes in the global competition between companies and locations often occur in relation to closing down and liquidating local firms and job loss. In some places, transformation of the urban system to meet new endogenous and exogenous requirements takes place successfully, especially if the location is considered an attractive area for settlement by the population and businesses. However, rethinking urban development is not only necessary because of economic and demographic change. A shortage in worldwide fossil fuel resources and issues of climate change necessitate the adoption of a new stance towards the topic of energy. The current basis of creation and consumption of energy is considered untenable from an economic, social, and ecological perspective.[1] At this stage, urban regions all over the world can and must make a significant contribution, in order to meet sustainability targets, particularly in view of the uninterrupted and increasing population influx to cities. Target agreements on the reduction of greenhouse gases and increased energy efficiency have been made on international and national levels in recent years and incorporated in legislation. While this indicates that the need for action has seemingly been recognised, the subject of sustainable urban development still lacks a systematic structure.

Towards an understanding of space

Sustainable urban development should be considered beyond the aspects of design and energy efficiency. It should make space usable as a catalyst for activities in an urban environment, and thereby create places with good living conditions.[2] Built space is only a dimension of space in this context, which is increasingly influenced by morphologically discontinuous relations of scale and location, due to globalisation and mobility. As part of the environment, built space can be considered the 'coagulated' result of previous negotiation processes within urban space. The significance of built space lies in the regulation of activities and perception of human beings and is characterised by a persistence that transcends the time of its creation. These patterns of use,[3] developed in the course of utilising the built city, are themselves part of ongoing negotiation processes.[4] Therefore, place itself is not a product that can be completed or delineated, but is always in the process of formation,[5] particularly due to the time lag between cause and effect in urban design. Space as field in which different forces manifest their effects is in constant feedback with the habitus of utilisation.[6] The field is constituted by the overlapping and penetration of various sets of interaction on a local level. Built space stands out here because of its relative permanence. The increased mobility of people and capital, and the associ-

For further aspects of social and societal change cf. Back to Being Social » *p. 60, 68*, *Trend Predictions* » *p. 102*, *Living Ergonomics* » *p. 123*, *Research Initiative 'Future Building'* » *p. 137*

1

OECD/International Energy Agency (IEA): World Energy Outlook. Executive Summary. Paris 2008

2

Williams, Katie; Burton, Elizabeth; Jenks, Mike (eds.): Achieving Sustainable Urban Form. London/ New York 2000

3

Bourdieu, Pierre; Wacquant, Loïc: 'Reflexive Anthropologie.' [Reflexive Anthropology.] Frankfurt/M. 1996

4

Löw, Martina: 'Raumsoziologie.' [Sociology of Space.] Frankfurt/M. 2001; Massey, Doreen: World City. Cambridge 2007

5

Cresswell, Tim: Geographies of Mobilities. Practices, Spaces, Subjects. London 2011

6

See note 3

For perspectives on urbanity and urban development cf. Parametric Design Systems » *p. 54*, *Back to Being Social* » *p. 66*

7

Castells, Manuel: Space of Flows – der Raum der Ströme. In: Stefan Bollmann (ed.), 'Kursbuch Stadt. Stadtleben und Stadtkultur an der Jahrtausendwende.' [Urban Life and Urban Culture at the Turn of the Century.] Stuttgart 1999, p. 39–81

8

Massey 2007, see note 4

9

Boudon, Philippe: The Point of View of Measurement in Architectural Conception. From Questions of Scale to Scale as Question. In: Nordic Journal of Architectural Research 01/1999, p. 7–18

10

Feldtkeller, Christoph (ed.): 'Der architektonische Raum: eine Fiktion. Annäherung an eine funktionale Betrachtung.' [Architectural Space: a Fiction. Approximation to a Functional Contemplation.] Bauwelt Fundamente 83, Braunschweig/Wiesbaden 1989; Schumacher, Patrick: Spatializing the Complexities of Contemporary Business Organization. In: Steele, Brett (ed.): Corporate Fields. New Office Environments by the AA D[R]L. London 2005

11

Lefebvre, Henri: The Production of Space. Oxford/Cambridge 1991

For questions concerning energy and handling of resources cf. » p. 77 as well as Parametric Design Systems » p. 52, Understanding Buildings as Systems » p. 82–93, Common Sense Instead of High Tech » p. 94, Building Processes of Tomorrow » p. 125, Collaboration of Industry and Research » p. 130, Research Initiative 'Future Building' » p. 136, 139ff.

ated definition of local as a differentiation of global necessitate a relational perspective, which considers exchange relationships between locations as space-defining.[7] Therefore, an individual location can not be detached from its network of exchange relationships, it rather constitutes a field of interactions. The local level is the individual manifestation and place of origin of mutually pervasive logics of networks[8] and remains part of a singular environment.

Thus, a primary challenge lies in the definition of the level of scale that should be used to make physical interventions in the city effective,[9] in addition to the spatial design that is based on topologically effective morphological and functional relations or actively stimulates these.[10] This results in a simultaneous dissolution of the divisions between building design and urban planning, which are both subject to questions on system boundaries to similar extents. However, these boundaries retain their significance in the urban environment of everyday life.[11] Thereby, they create a framework for the development of concepts of sustainability.

Problem field

The complex framework conditions of abandoned, centrally located industrial areas are a challenge for all parties involved. Existing structures in the vicinity and on the respective sites require an integrated planning method that takes into account both demand and supply of space. The expected interactions are significant, and any strategy has to take into consideration specifically local aspects. The factors that can impact the results of a dynamic model of urban development have to be identified and their development has to be estimated. Top priority is given to appropriate handling of resources. An efficient energy supply of an urban block may, for instance, be closely related to the size of a district heating network. A drop in demand, e.g. due to improving energy efficiency, affects the efficiency of the overall system. Hence – despite local savings – this does not necessarily give rise to the desired positive effect.[12] Therefore, improvements in such systems have to be closely linked to developments in other areas, in order to take into consideration the future energy demand of existing buildings and new buildings. Yet, due to issues of ownership, directly influencing such processes is often not possible. Still, long-term scenarios can significantly improve an understanding of such interactions and help develop system-relevant regulators.

A long-term perspective is similarly required for new construction. The availability of plots of land that, as fenced-in industrial areas, have all but vanished from public perception, offer opportunities to re-program the urban code – morphologically, functionally, and socially. In view of the supra-regional nature of the challenges of globalisation, but also the competition for knowledge and for human and investment capital, this can be considered a chance to compare and evaluate alternative development scenarios. On the one hand, material and non-material resources have to be recognised as typical local characteristics in an urban development context. On the other hand, they have to be made useable. Application of standard solutions such as compact and mixed use development[13] alone are insufficient to achieve possible potentials. What is required is the courage to plan step-by-step within the framework of an integrated strategy. Long-term orientation requires visionary thinking. Supported by modern technology, it identifies synergy and conflict potentials, while the associated strategic framework remains adaptive and flexible enough to incorporate changes.[14] The decision on which levels of scale are important and applicable is a decisive step on the way towards efficient realisation of sustainability targets, provided this leads to anchoring the new in the already existing. Therefore, focus is not only on local improvement, but also on a deliberate promotion of the synergy effects of different dimensions of sustainability, in order to achieve a maximum effect with relatively limited government intervention. The potential lies in the mobilisation of existing structures – physical and non-physical – and the resulting integration in a local context, facilitating social, ecological, and economic sustainability.[15]

Occurrence and identification

Most European cities are already 'completely' built. Therefore, the rare opportunities to plan major interrelated interventions gain strategic importance for the adaptation of cities to changes and influencing their international ranking. The intervention that may be large, yet spatially limited should ideally have an influence beyond its immediate surroundings and act as a stimulus for the entire city. Achieving such an effect requires a collective understanding of the problem. The as-is situation in terms of the current overlap of physical and non-physical factors of spatial relevance – the resources – of the city and of the site, requires decoding.[16] On the basis of existing qualities, means, and instruments, the challenges of the future can best be met by selective use of these resources as potentials for development. Such potentials are created by an overlap of the supply side with the demand side of urban development in specific cases. Many such areas exist in central locations all across Europe. Examples include HafenCity Hamburg, Zurich-West, London Kings Cross, Nuremberg-West and Munich-East – inner-city areas of a significant size in the process of redefinition (76|2).

While the relocation and closure of industrial facilities and the associated availability of their respective sites opens up a potential for reallocation, it is the specifically local demand for residential, office, and free space that makes such a reallocation lucrative. Companies of the knowledge economy profit from the central location of these areas, as well as

12

Koziol, Matthias: 'Herausforderungen energetischer Stadterneuerung. Schlüsse aus dem deutschen Forschungsfeld.' [Challenges of Urban Energy Renewal. Conclusions from the German Field of Research.] In: Bauwelt 12/2011, p. 22–31

13

See note 2

14

Harvey, David: Between Space and Time. Reflections on the Geographical Imagination. In: Annals of the Association of American Geographers 03/1990, p. 17

15

German Bundestag: The Concept of Sustainability. From Vision to Reality. Final Report of the 13th German Bundestag's Enquete Commission on the 'Protection of Humanity and the Environment: Objectives and General Conditions of Sustainable Development'. Berlin 1998

For the potential of use changes and renovations cf. Back to Being Social » p. 61f., Understanding Buildings as Systems » p. 84, Common Sense Instead of High Tech » p. 99, Building Processes of Tomorrow » p. 127, Research Initiative 'Future Building' » p. 137

16

Thierstein, Alain; Langer Wioco, Anna; Förster, Agnes: 'Ein Wirkungsmodell für Stadtentwicklung: Kreativ, attraktiv, wettbewerbsfähig.' [An Impact Model for Urban Development: Creative, Attractive, Competitive.] In: Koch, Florian; Frey, Oliver (eds.): 'Die Zukunft der Europäischen Stadt. Stadtpolitik, Stadtplanung und Stadtgesellschaft im Wandel.' [The Future of the European City. Changes in Urban Policy, Urban Planning, and Urban Society.] Wiesbaden 2011, p. 103–118

17

Florida, Richard: The Rise of the Creative Class. New York 2002; Sassen, Saskia: The Global City. New York, London, Tokyo. Vol. 1. Princeton, N.J. 1991

18

Thierstein, Alain; Wiese, Anne: Attracting Talents. 'Metropolregionen im Wettbewerb um Humankapital.' [Metropolitan Regions in Competition for Human Capital.] In: RegioPol, Zeitschrift für Regionalwissenschaft [Journal of Regional Science], 1–2/2011, p. 127–137

19

Howells, Jeremy: Knowledge, Innovation and Location. In: Bryson, John R. et al. (eds.): Knowledge, Space, Economy. London/New York 2000, p. 50–62

20

Berking, Helmuth; Löw, Martina (eds.): 'Die Eigenlogik der Städte.' [Intrinsic Logic of Cities] Frankfurt 2008

21

Amin, Ash; Thrift, Nigel: Cities Reimagining the Urban. Cambridge 2002

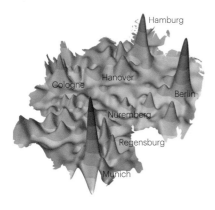

74|1 **Migration statistics** for persons age 18–29 between 2000 and 2009 in Germany

their close proximity to customers, competitors, and educational institutions in metropolitan regions.[17] They are among those centres that are particularly attractive to young people, while population numbers in rural regions continue to decline.[18] This shift in favour of a small number of cities in Germany accompanied by population shrinkage in rural regions is illustrated in figure 74|1.

This process is further advanced by the increasing importance of production, distribution, and application of knowledge within the economic system.[19] Heavily knowledge-based processes and services are essential competition factors of European companies and cities. Therefore, the relative location – resulting from the absolute favourability of the location within a networked world – gains strategic significance. Yet, the local supply and demand situations differ in each individual case. From a relational point of view, London is an established global location, while Zurich is particularly significant on a European level. Hamburg and Munich are important hubs in a national network of urban regions, while Nuremberg has a more regional significance. This also leads to differing requirements with regard to sustainable development, as shown by the space-relevant indicators settlement area and traffic area, as well as average commuting time to work (75|1).

These indicators are both the result and starting point of urban development. Thus, the existing energy supply network and the transport infrastructure enormously influence the potential of climate-friendly urban renewal processes. The above-mentioned areas, for instance, differ significantly in terms of accessibility. While Kings Cross (currently still under construction) benefits tremendously from its connection to the international high-speed rail network, HafenCity Hamburg (large parts of which are already completed) is still waiting to be connected to the underground railway system. This means that a trip to Cologne from either location takes about 4 hours and 20 minutes – an interesting circumstance for multi-national corporations, the target group of many cities. The associated requirements and profiles of users constitute an important contribution to the functioning of the area and its chance of prospering as part of the whole city. The objective of a liveable city is closely linked to these profiles, and then determine the activity in the city. The activity is the result of a superimposition of different profiles, which in turn give rise to specific space-time intervals, as illustrated by figure 77|1.

Families, employees, students, and tourists are characterised by different utilisation patterns in space and time. The evaluation of diverse scenarios as part of strategy development is based on an analysis of the supply and demand situation of various user groups, and therefore, directly influences the achievement of sustainability targets. User integration in an early planning stage allows development of specific local solutions, thereby creating maximum added value.

Such urban renewal processes may last several generations and demand a high degree of interdisciplinarity and comprehensive planning methodology. In this respect, an understanding of the local intrinsic logic[20] is just as important as the analysis of global ranking.[21] An evaluation within the scope of strategy development that integrates top-down and bottom-up is decisive.[22] At the same time, a flexible framework needs to be established in order to permit and integrate changes of endogenous or exogenous origin.

Concept

Development within existing structures is fundamentally different from greenfield development, especially in the case of sustainability. For the former, inclusion of the surrounding context is imperative. Almost as important for reaching sustainability goals are the participants involved, especially planners, investors, and other interest groups with their specific visions and potentials. They are the ones who promote changes in companies and organisations by constantly aligning their actions with the environment.

Our concept of the city as a relational structure of different qualities and of varying range integrates the three components built city, used city, and organisation of the city within the term 'resources'. The aim is to reconcile interests between the individual and the community in the sense of a 'liveable city'.[23] In an ideal case, the project creates recognisable and identity-generating places by embedding it within interdependencies that extend beyond the particular area. The problem fields give rise to new spatial boundaries, the potentials and deficits of which are analysed in a transdisciplinary process.[24] Figure 79|2 illustrates this approach as part of the project plan for Nuremberg-West.

Such a transdisciplinary design process requires an additional expenditure with regard to communication and coordination within the team, as well as a rethinking process as far as conventional planning practice is concerned. However, the tools required for this process are available: modelling and scenario techniques are perfectly suitable for the calculation and illustration of trend projections. Virtual project platforms offer document access to all those involved in the project, and visualisations elucidate highly complex interrelationships without requiring expert knowledge.

Particularly with regard to the diverse interdependencies in existing structures, trend projection via scenarios provides a way of offering actors in urban planning information on the likely effects of decisions, and thus, capacity to influence the planning of systems. However, prior to illustrating scenarios, a complex analysis of the baseline situation is necessary, in order to be able to display the sensitivities of the system and to formulate hypotheses on the boundary conditions according to

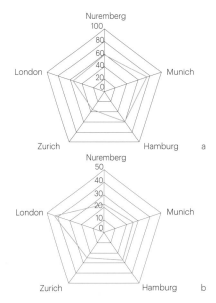

75|1 Comparative analysis of space-relevant indicators; a: proportion of settlement area and traffic area (in percent); b: average commuting time to work (in minutes)

22

Penrose, Edith: The Theory of the Growth of the Firm. Oxford 1959

23

UrbanUnlimited: Hardware-Software-Orgware; http://www.urbanunlimited.nl/uu/uu.nsf/03/FA1C089E2BDB115BC1256AFB0052C464?opendocument (accessed on 15.06.2011)

24

Mayer, Hans-Norbert: 'Mit Projekten planen.' [Planning with Projects.] In: Dangschat, Oliver; Frey, Jens (eds.): 'Strategieorientierte Planung im kooperativen Staat.' [Strategy-Oriented Planning in a Cooperative State.] Wiesbaden 2008, p. 128–150

For parameters, methods, and application examples of trend research cf. Trend Predictions » p. 105, Building Processes of Tomorrow » p. 125, Collaboration of Industry and Research » p. 130

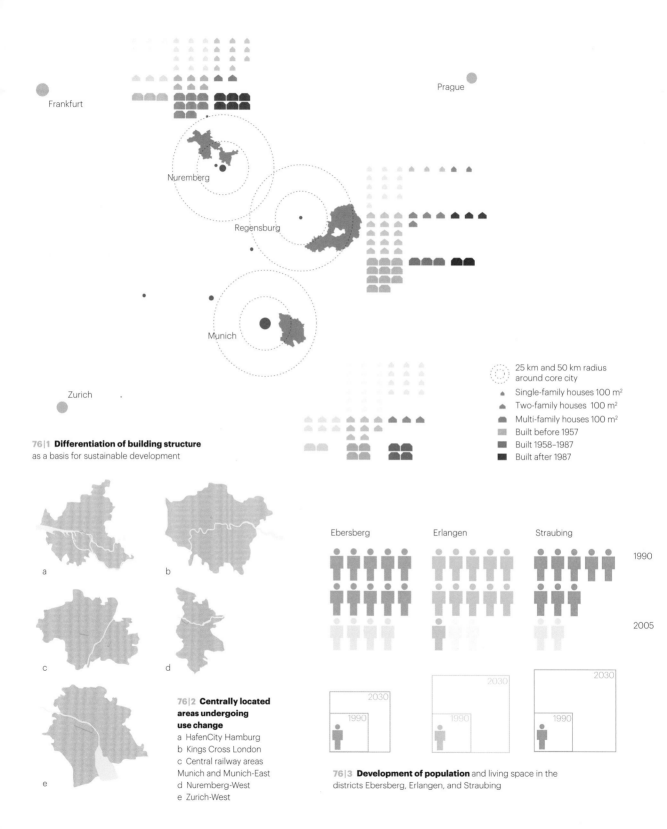

Frankfurt

Prague

Nuremberg

Regensburg

Munich

Zurich

76|1 **Differentiation of building structure**
as a basis for sustainable development

25 km and 50 km radius
around core city
▲ Single-family houses 100 m²
🏠 Two-family houses 100 m²
🏢 Multi-family houses 100 m²
Built before 1957
Built 1958–1987
Built after 1987

a

b

c

d

e

76|2 **Centrally located
areas undergoing
use change**
a HafenCity Hamburg
b Kings Cross London
c Central railway areas
Munich and Munich-East
d Nuremberg-West
e Zurich-West

Ebersberg   Erlangen   Straubing   1990

2005

2030   2030   2030
1990   1990   1990

76|3 **Development of population** and living space in the
districts Ebersberg, Erlangen, and Straubing

local circumstances. In this regard, the quality of the relation to the specific situation on site plays an important role and forms a basis for developing a strategy adapted to local conditions. For example, a bottom-up model for observing heating demand development scenarios that takes into account the different features of three Bavarian districts ('Landkreis') was created within the scope of a research project. The specific framework conditions of housing stock and other factors such as population development (76|3) are included according to region-specific calculations.[25] An illustration of the distribution of residential space for each building type (including one-family, two-family, and multi-family houses) in the typical building age groups indicates variations among baseline situations for the specific stock of residential buildings in each case (76|1). Differences in building structure can most easily be recognised when observing the proportion of single-family houses, which is particularly high in the Straubing-Bogen district, with a settlement density of 80 inhabitants per square kilometre.

In line with different building structures, significant differences can also be observed in the development of the average residential space per inhabitant for each of the districts under consideration. The average residential space in the Ebersberg district was 41.10 square metres in 2008, with as much as 47.20 square metres in Straubing-Bogen in the same year, which is mainly attributable to the very high proportion of single-family homes there.

In order to be able to observe the development of heating demand within scenarios, a stochastic simulation analysis based on the specific conditions was carried out. As result, important factors included the district-specific development of living space per inhabitant and the development of region-specific population figures.

As demonstrated by the trend projection of the heating demand in the scenarios for the three Bavarian districts, results vary significantly because of the great variation in the parameters of specific local situations. With approximately 200 kWh/m²a, the average heating demand in Straubing-Bogen in the year 2008 is about 29 percent above that in Ebersberg, with a recorded figure of 155 kWh/m²a. This means that Straubing-Bogen is the district with the highest savings potentials up to the year 2030. By use of a simulation of building development based on specific local characteristics, scenarios can be illustrated and need for action can be recognised in a clear and concise way (79|1).

Previous establishment of critical factors permits a quantitative calculation of the effects of interventions in the building fabric. This allows illustration of synergies and obstacles for achieving targets that can be helpful in the decision-making processes required for funding.

The spatial strategy is product and process at the same time. As a process, it is based on local administrative structures and on-site knowledge resources, which in turn structure the process through communication

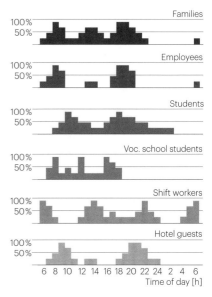

77|1 Varying **utilisation intensities** of urban space in the course of a day

25

Nemeth, Isabell: 'Methodenentwicklung zur Bestimmung von Potenzialen der Energieeffizienzsteigerung im Haushalts- und GHD-Sektor – Am Beispiel von drei Landkreisen in Bayern.' [Method Development for Determination of Potentials of Increasing Energy Efficiency in the Household and Business/Commerce/Services Sector – Exemplified by Three Districts in Bavaria.] Dissertation, TU Munich, 2011

For questions concerning energy and handling of resources cf. » *p. 72 as well as Parametric Design Systems* » *p. 52, Understanding Buildings as Systems* » *p. 82–93, Common Sense Instead of High Tech* » *p. 94, Building Processes of Tomorrow* » *p. 125, Collaboration of Industry and Research* » *p. 130, Research Initiative 'Future Building'* » *p. 136, 139ff.*

26

Healey, Patsy: Urban Complexity and
Spatial Strategies. Towards a
Relational Planning for Our Times.
London 2007

27

Sieverts, Thomas: 'Zwischenstadt.
Zwischen Ort und Welt, Raum
und Zeit, Stadt und Land.' [Neither
Urban Nor Rural. Between Local
and Global, Space and Time, Urban
and Rural.] Bauwelt Fundamente
118. Braunschweig/Wiesbaden 1997

Geographic Information Systems (GIS)
*are used for acquisition, processing,
organisation, analysis, and presentation
of space-related information. In addition to visualisation, GIS provide many
functions for analysis of geographic
data.*

cf.: Hauschild, Moritz; Karzel, Rüdiger: 'Digitale
Prozesse' [Digital Processes]. Munich 2010, p. 105

patterns and promote development.[26] A first step involves evaluation of
needs and potentials, as well as the possibilities of urban renewal. The
aim is to develop alternative scenarios and new approaches that represent an analytical basis for creating flexible and robust urban development concepts, without formulating an obligatory master plan. A second
phase serves to develop resulting strategic guidelines.

Conclusions

Urban development has become a complex field of interactive processes.
On the one hand, this is due to a change in boundaries and levels of
scale. On the other hand, the reason is an addition of new influence factors. This increases the need for a transdisciplinary and forward-looking
modus operandi. Limited financial resources and already existing cities
in Europe restrict the options for sustainable and viable urban renewal.
This makes each individual intervention all the more important for activating strategically relevant physical and non-physical resources with
regard to sustainability. Nevertheless, if coordination of the innumerable
small interventions is successful, the result within the European city will
be significant.[27]

Handling these limited possibilities requires a rethinking of existing planning methods, if the multi-faceted challenges resulting from a relational
understanding of space and location are to be met. An effective combination of relevant knowledge already existing in theory and practice and in
public and private institutions needs to be promoted in a targeted way to
avoid conflicts. Therefore, the process design itself becomes the subject
of a multi-dimensional discourse, with the aim of tailoring the procedure
as a whole to the task at hand in an optimal way, and of identifying topical interfaces beyond the boundaries of specific disciplines. The conceptual framework established in this manner is derived from the results of
the analysis and allows actors to classify the relevance of their involvement with regard to the respective levels of scale. The utilisation of scenario techniques and Geographic Information Systems (GIS) can, in
combination with other methods, support this aim by making the consequences of individual contributions and the interconnections between
them more comprehensible. The goal is to enable the network of participants to develop innovative approaches and to encourage a negotiation
process that allows the solution created to be integrated in the field that
encompasses various levels of scale and activity.

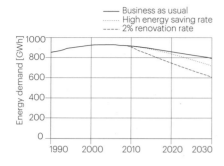

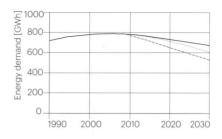

79|1 **Energy demand forecast** based on option for action; a: District of Ebersberg; b: District of Straubing-Bogen

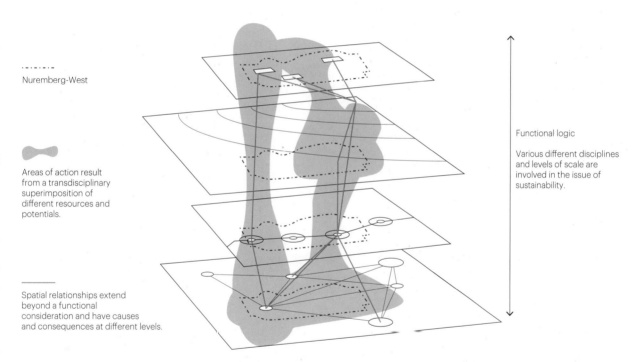

Nuremberg-West

Areas of action result from a transdisciplinary superimposition of different resources and potentials.

Spatial relationships extend beyond a functional consideration and have causes and consequences at different levels.

Functional logic

Various different disciplines and levels of scale are involved in the issue of sustainability.

79|2 **Interaction of different types of functional logic** and different spatial scale levels for sustainable development of Nuremberg-West

Understanding Buildings as Systems – Location as Identity Generator

Text Anja Thierfelder, Matthias Schuler

Since the invention of mechanical ventilation and cooling systems, knowledge on buildings as breathing structures has been all but forgotten – after all, every house can be given the desired indoor climate using building services equipment.

However, resources are finite worldwide, and as indicated by the Intergovernmental Panel on Climate Change (IPCC) in the Valencia Report 2007, emissions have a far-reaching impact. Together with the global rise in energy prices, these facts form the basis of a rethinking process with regard to the shapes, structures, materials, and orientation of buildings. Ideal adaptation of architecture and building designs to local climatic conditions allows them to be turned into systems that breathe. In that case, natural ventilation, illumination, and air conditioning of such buildings may be possible throughout several months of the year or even the entire year. If the building itself represents the basic system and functionality of the building doesn't rely on mechanical equipment, then a comfortable living and working environment can be created for the user. Therefore, the starting point of all planning is the place or site of building, or more broadly speaking, the locality. This makes sense, since architecture is not created in a void or empty space, but in an urbanised and landscaped environment. And every environment has its typical characteristics, its genius loci.

The Norwegian architect and architecture critic Christian Norberg-Schulz was convinced that the phenomena of architecture cannot be described by using only analytical, scientific terms. He set out his understanding of the phenomenology of architecture in 'Genius Loci', published in 1976.[1] According to Norberg-Schulz, a place is always a totality made up of particular things with material substance, shape, surface, and colour; a place is a qualitative total phenomenon, also referred to as atmosphere or character. Orientation and identification are prerequisites for finding your way around a place. Orientation implies constitution of space, and therefore identification is only possible if the place has an unambiguous, clearly defined character, a genius loci.[2]

Norberg-Schulz's book received significant attention – the term genius loci was ubiquitous for a long time, yet almost forgotten later on. The resuscitation of the term is attributable to the general weariness of a worldwide uniformity resulting from so-called globalisation. Once more, it appears in international architectural discourse more frequently and in conjunction with terms such as identity or authenticity.

Jean Nouvel is one of the most prominent contemporary and internationally active architects and recipient of the Pritzker Architecture Prize 2008. In his 2005 'Louisiana Manifesto'[3] he laments that architecture annihilates, banalises, and violates places. Commercial interests accentuate dominant architecture, the type that claims not to require any context. Nouvel talks about a confrontation between practitioners of situation-related architecture and profiteers of decontextualised architecture. He demands: "We must [...] establish sensitive, poetic rules, approaches that will speak of colours, essences, characters, [...] the specificities of the rain, wind, sea and mountain [...]. The ideology of the specific aspires to autonomy, to the use of the resources of the place and the time, to the privileging of the non-material. How can we use what is here and nowhere else? How can we differentiate without caricaturing? How can we achieve depth? [...] Architecture means transformation, organising the mutations of what is already there [...] Architecture should be seen as the modification of a physical, atomic, biological continuum [...] Architecture means the adaptation of the condition of a place to a given time by the willpower, desire and knowledge of human beings. We never do this alone."

1

Norberg-Schultz, Christian: Genius Loci. Towards a Phenomenology of Architecture. New York 1991

2

Führ, Eduard:'genius loci'. Phänomen oder Phantom? ['genius loci'. Phenomenon or Phantom?] In: Wolkenkuckucksheim, 02/1998

Established by the World Meteorological Organisation (WMO) and the United Nations Environment Programme (UNEP) in 1988, the Intergovernmental Panel on Climate Change *(IPCC) is the leading international body for assessment of climate change. It does not conduct any research projects, but is an intergovernmental body for exchange of knowledge between scientists and other representatives from over 100 states. The results of scientific studies are collected and analysed by the organisation.*

cf: http://www.bpb.de/themen/W4XKVV,0,0,20_Jahre_Weltklimarat_.html (accessed on 20.10.2011)

3

Jean Nouvel: Louisiana Manifesto. Ed. by Michael Juul Holm. Louisiana Museum of Modern Art. 2008

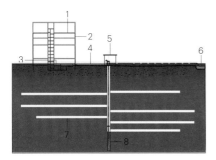

84|1 Energy concept of the Zollverein School, Essen

1 Thermal mass activation
2 Exterior wall with active insulation
3 Fresh air heating
4 Local heat pipe
5 Heat exchange system (pit water/water)
6 River Emscher
7 1,200-metre-deep shaft
8 Pit water (approx. 35 °C)

84|2 Active insulation permits **monolithic concrete walls** with a thickness of only 30 centimetres. Zollverein School, Essen

For the potential of use changes and renovations cf. Back to being Social » p. 61f., Sustainable Urban Development » p. 73, Common Sense Instead of High Tech » p. 99, Building Processes of Tomorrow » p. 127, Research Initiative 'Future Building' » p. 137

Both the architectural theorist Norberg-Schulz and the architect Nouvel talk about the genius loci, the spirit of a place, as a starting point for substantial and place-related architecture. We, as climate engineers, begin every project with a direct, measurable, and location-specific approach. Every location has unique climate data, which are not identical for any two places on earth. Determination and analysis of these parameters is the first step of our work and a direct prerequisite for all further decisions.

However, a location analysis is not limited to determination of measurable weather data – we are, in a sense, also searching for the spirit of the place in our own special way: What are the potentials offered by the building site and the neighbourhood? How can these be used creatively and effectively for the planned construction project? What special features stand out? What should be protected or preserved? Which improvements would be desirable? Which intervention is expected to result in what consequences?

Climate concepts deemed to be appropriate for the location and building project are created on the basis of these findings. The most impressive projects are often those characterised by an unmistakable relation to the location; they make use of a unique technical solution that cannot be transferred to another place. Climate engineering can accentuate the special quality of the architecture in such cases and contribute to the identity of a place.

Project examples

Zollverein School, Essen (D) 2006, SANAA From 1851 until 1986 the former Zollverein coal mine was important for generation of energy required by the steel production industry in the Ruhr area. Since its decommission, water has been drained from the disused galleries at depths of up to 1000 metres to keep the pit dry for possible later use of the facilities. The pit water, pumped up at a flow rate of 600 m³/h, has a temperature of approximately 29 °C throughout the year. The climate in Essen is moderate, with temperatures rarely above or below a range of 0 °C to 30 °C.

The Zollverein School project at the perimeter of the Zollverein coal mine is part of extensive restructuring efforts in the Ruhr area. The architectural office SANAA from Tokyo won the international competition held for this purpose with the design of a simple concrete cube structure featuring a striking arrangement of window openings. Utilisation of the pit water as a location-specific energy source allowed realisation of monolithic concrete walls with a thickness of only 30 centimetres (84|2). A completely new concept of 'active insulation' was developed. This involves pit water flowing through plastic pipes embedded in the monolithic concrete wall and thereby heating the wall. This 'active' thermal insulation ensures that the surface temperature of the interior face of the wall is always above 18 °C, and therefore within the comfort range of a heated room. The exterior of the wall is not thermally insulated, which means that about 80 percent of the thermal energy is lost to the environment. However, this is tolerable, because the energy source is CO_2-independent and absolutely free. In addition, the construction of the monolithic wall with integrated pipe system cost much less than a comparable double-shell concrete wall, and therefore saved an amount of money that was greater than the expenses for the pit water system. This was one of the main reasons why realisation of this geothermal system was possible for the Zollverein School, while a similar system was not implemented in a neighbouring building, for which the investment costs would not have been covered by the savings.

Based on the idea of using the free potential of renewable energy in the pit water for heating the building, a secondary water circuit with heat exchanger was installed at the top of the mine shaft as a district heat source for the Zollverein School. This secondary circuit is necessary, because of the poor quality of the pit water. The heat exchanger is accessible for regular maintenance to ensure reliable function. Water analyses and material tests had to be carried out before beginning construction work to verify the functionality of the system.

This unique energy concept (84|1) is based on the utilisation of location-specific conditions. It represents a solution that is only feasible for the Zollverein School in Essen, while at the same time referring to the local historical tradition of coal mining. Further ideas for utilisation of the pit water as a local, CO_2-free energy source already exist.

Lycée Charles de Gaulle, Damascus (SYR) 2009, Ateliers Lion   Transsolar was commissioned to develop a climate concept for a new French school in Damascus, together with the architects at Ateliers Lion. Specifications included adaptation to the local weather conditions – a dry desert climate with hot days and cold nights.

The school complex consists of several small buildings, which contain two stacked class rooms and are connected through courtyards with greenery (85|2). The aim was to find a low-tech solution for ventilation and air conditioning of the class rooms, and propose a new interpretation of traditional architecture by using local materials.

Wind-supported solar chimneys allow natural cross-ventilation of the class rooms (85|1). They are equipped with polycarbonate panels on one side in order to collect solar radiation and reinforce the stack effect. During the day, fresh air enters the class rooms either directly from the shady micro-climate of the courtyards, or pre-cooled within miniature earth ducts embedded as pipes in the floor slabs. Ventilation can be controlled by means of adjustable dampers.

At night, the thermal mass of the chimneys radiates the thermal energy stored during the day, resulting in cool night air being drawn

Winter day

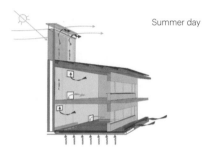

Summer day

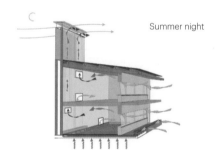

Summer night

85|1 Wind-supported solar chimneys ensure natural ventilation of classrooms. Lycée Charles de Gaulle, Damascus

85|2 Small buildings each containing two stacked classrooms connected via **courtyards with greenery**. Lycée Charles de Gaulle, Damascus

into the building through open windows and piping. This leads to cooling off the thermal mass of the class rooms and lowers the room temperatures for the next day. In summer, the courtyard is shaded from sunlight during the day, while remaining open at night to allow cooling by emitting heat skywards. The reverse procedure in winter aims to store daytime solar gains and then prevent their loss into the clear night sky.

Deutsche Post, Bonn (D) 2003, Murphy/Jahn Architects The Deutsche Post was privatised during planning of its new headquarters in Bonn. This meant that the former state-owned company was at liberty to decide whether it would remain in the former German capital, instead of moving to Berlin and following the federal government's relocation effort. As one of the leading logistics companies in the world, its new headquarters was expected to represent an innovative contribution to corporate identity. The competition requirements specified high user comfort and a high-quality working environment, in conjunction with low operating and energy costs.

The site is located directly along the banks of the Rhine, which means that the groundwater level is very high because of riverbank filtration. Due to an average ground temperature of 10 °C, groundwater wells only 30 metres in depth provide cold water with a maximum temperature of 15 °C, even on summer days. The location of the new building in the middle of a park landscape offers ideal conditions for openable facades.

The curved shape of the building responds to the typical local wind directions (86|1). It offers minimal wind resistance and allows ventilation of the building by making use of adjacent pressure differences. Because of their north-south orientation, the double facades have two different geometries and vary in depth: smooth towards the north, and gently sloping towards the south for better ventilation and higher solar gains. Pressure differences in the double skin facade are equalised through centrally controlled openings in the external skin, so that users can open the windows of the inner facade skin regardless of weather conditions. The cavity between the facade skins offers wind protection for the external solar shading system and allows pressure regulation via the facade openings. It also facilitates the distribution of fresh air, while the sky gardens function as vent stacks. As result of this system, vertical ducts for ventilation and infiltration were not required, permitting maximisation of space efficiency.

Masdar City Masterplan, Abu Dhabi (UAE) 2007, Foster + Partners Abu Dhabi, the capital of the United Arab Emirates, is located on the Persian Gulf, which heats up to about 35 °C in summer due to the shallow waters of the coastal regions. The sea introduces warm and humid air into the city from the north-west, with temperatures of up to

86|1 **Deutsche Post** headquarters, Bonn

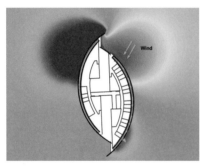

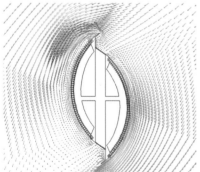

86|2 **Flow simulation results** show wind pressures along the facade. The concept of a corridor double-skin facade, allowing natural ventilation of the offices, was developed based on these. Deutsche Post, Bonn

47 °C in summer. Until the 1960s the location near the sea was only used for pearl diving from October to April, because of the pleasant weather conditions in the city during those months. During the summer heat, people traditionally moved to Al Ain in the mountains in an attempt to at least escape from the humidity.

Masdar Development, the UAE government's vision of the world's first climate-neutral city, takes into account the conditions prevailing in this perhaps sunniest place on the planet, which boasts very high solar gains of up to 2.00 to 2.20 kWh/m²a. Typically, thermal comfort in outdoor areas is imperative in urban development. However, this isn't the case in modern Abu Dhabi – pedestrians simply 'melt' away while crossing from one side of an avenue to the other.

Due to the climatic specifications, and based on numerous simulation results, as well as wind tunnel test models, the masterplan suggests measures for maintaining temperatures in the streets below those beyond the city, while taking into account the local macro- and micro-climate. The buildings themselves and their specific orientation shade the narrow streets, and short street lengths prevent unpleasant wind effects typical for canyon-like street systems (87|1). Part of the efforts to achieve an 'urban cold island effect' rather than the familiar urban heat island effect involved a reinterpretation of historic wind towers (87|2) – to ventilate the streets at night and protect them from the hot summer wind during the day. Linear parks intersect the city from north-west to

87|1 Limited length and breadth of streets prevents hot fall winds. Masdar City, Abu Dhabi

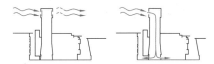

87|2 New interpretation of historic wind towers: for wind protection during the day and for ventilation of the streets at night. Masdar City, Abu Dhabi

Urban heat island effect *The higher air and surface temperatures in settlement areas compared to surrounding areas are referred to as Urban Heat Islands (UHI). Their intensity depends on the weather situation and is closely linked to the time of day and year.*

cf: Kuttler, Wilhelm: 'Stadtklima. Teil 2: Phänomene und Wirkungen.' [Urban Climate. Part 2: Main Features and Effects.] University of Duisburg-Essen, Institute of Geography, Dept. of Applied Climatology and Landscape Ecology. 2004

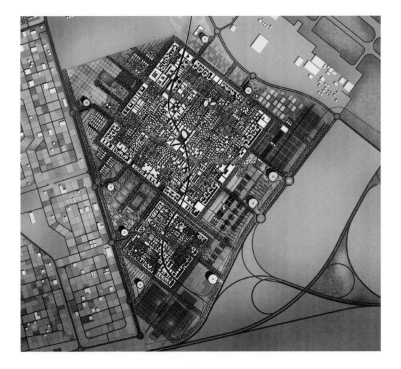

87|3 Narrow parks intersect the city similar to **green fingers**. Masdar City, Abu Dhabi

88|1 and 88|2 Eight residential towers connected by bridges, arranged around a **central park and water landscape** as public space.
Linked Hybrid, Beijing

Urban heat island effect *The higher air and surface temperatures in settlement areas compared to surrounding areas are referred to as Urban Heat Islands (UHI). Their intensity depends on the weather situation and is closely linked to the time of day and year.*

cf: Kuttler, Wilhelm: 'Stadtklima. Teil 2: Phänomene und Wirkungen.' [Urban Climate. Part 2: Main Features and Effects.] University of Duisburg-Essen, Institute of Geography, Dept. of Applied Climatology and Landscape Ecology, 2004

east similar to green fingers (87|3). On the one hand, they allow basic ventilation, and on the other hand, they capture the cooler easterly winds through their orientation. These measures for creating an urban environment with thermal as well as visual comfort have resulted in completely different outdoor conditions outside of the buildings in the city – shady and cool – compared to those in the desert surrounding the city. This has a direct and positive influence on the energy consumption in Masdar.

Linked Hybrid Building, Beijing (RC) 2009, Steven Holl Architects

China's rapidly growing economy results in an enormous demand for high-quality housing in the city centres. Environmental damage in follow of economic growth and limited energy resources force the country to invest in major efforts with regard to energy-efficient buildings. The Linked Hybrid complex is located directly next to two residential towers based on a sustainable design and built by the project developer Modern Group in collaboration with the architects Baumschlager Eberle. This project sets the ecological standard within this part of the city.

Steven Holl Architects designed eight residential towers with 750 apartments for 2500 inhabitants for Linked Hybrid, arranged around a central park and water landscape with a pond as a public space (88|1 and 88|2). The connecting bridges on the 23rd floor are semi-private areas offering residents facilities such as a spa, pool, gym, art gallery, and café. The architectural concept incorporates public access to the ground floor space, accommodating shops a restaurant, and a school and kindergarten. The park landscape between the towers is accessible from each of these to prevent the impression of a 'gated community'. Nevertheless, the complex satisfies the security requirements of the residents. A pond covering 7800 square metres represents the element water – a scarce resource in Beijing – and is fed by grey water from the apartments.

Beijing's average outdoor temperature of 12 °C allows utilisation of the ground as a natural source of heating and cooling. For the project, 600 geothermal heat exchangers were installed at a depth of 100 metres. These serve as a source of cooling or heating energy for reversible heat pumps, as well as for direct cooling at certain times of the year. Minimisation of external loads is an important prerequisite for such an energy-efficient concept. This is achieved by means of a highly insulated building envelope, windows that can be opened, mechanical ventilation and infiltration based on a displacement ventilation system with central heat recovery, as well as integration of external, wind-proof sun protection of exposed facades. To make use of the natural ground temperature, activation of the thermal mass of unclad ceiling slabs was used for basic indoor air conditioning. However, the cooling demand exceeds the heating demand of the building, despite equipment with all available energy-saving functions. This means that the geothermal system causes the ground temperature of the area in which the borehole heat exchangers are installed to increase within the course of the year. In spring, a regeneration of the ground temperature is achieved using the surface of the pond as a natural cooling unit.

Manitoba Hydro Place, Winnipeg (CDN) 2009, KPMB Architects

Winnipeg has a population of over 500,000, is the coldest city in the world, but the sunniest location in Canada, with the hottest and most humid summers in the country (which is also reflected in the largest per capita number of air-conditioning systems). Temperature fluctuations of up to 70 °C occur during the course of the year, with temperatures below -35 °C in winter and above 35 °C in summer.

Relocating the new Manitoba Hydro head office with its 64,800 square metres from the outskirts to the inner city of Winnipeg was intentional. The new building of Canada's fourth-largest energy supplier is intended to represent a quantum leap in terms of energy efficiency and reduction of CO_2 emissions. In addition, it is supposed to contribute towards a revitalisation of the inner city by providing jobs for 2,500 employees. A primary aim was to reduce energy consumption to a figure of 60 percent below the national standard. An Integrated Design Process (IDP) was a prerequisite for realising the ambitious targets of the project, which combine aesthetics, sustainable design, and energy efficiency.

Achieving energy savings of 60 percent involved maximising the utilisation of passive systems and including a basic mechanical ventilation system, as well as natural ventilation through openable windows. The shape and dimensions of the office tower allow optimal use of solar and wind energy. Building operation modes are based on three seasonal types – winter, summer, and spring/autumn. The 'merging' of the two towers in the north opens them up towards the south (89|1) in order to make use of solar intake and strong southern winds typical for Winnipeg. This part of the building is divided into stacked, six-story atrium spaces that function as solar collectors. In combination with the solar chimney, they also serve as the 'lung' of the building and ensure a maximum supply of fresh air (90|1).

This project illustrates the value of integrated design for reaching environmental and ecological goals, as well as emphasising that much more can be achieved through such processes: architecture that creates healthy and high quality working environments, initiates the activation of public space, and contributes to the quality of urban life – and thereby represents an investment in the future.

Charles Hostler Student Center, American University of Beirut (AUB), Beirut (RL) 2008, Vincent James Associates Architects   The American University of Beirut (AUB) was founded as a private, independent, and non-denominational higher education institution in 1866. At

89|1 Towards the south, the tower has three **six-story winter gardens** designed to utilize abundant sunlight and strong southern winds in winter. Manitoba Hydro Place, Winnipeg

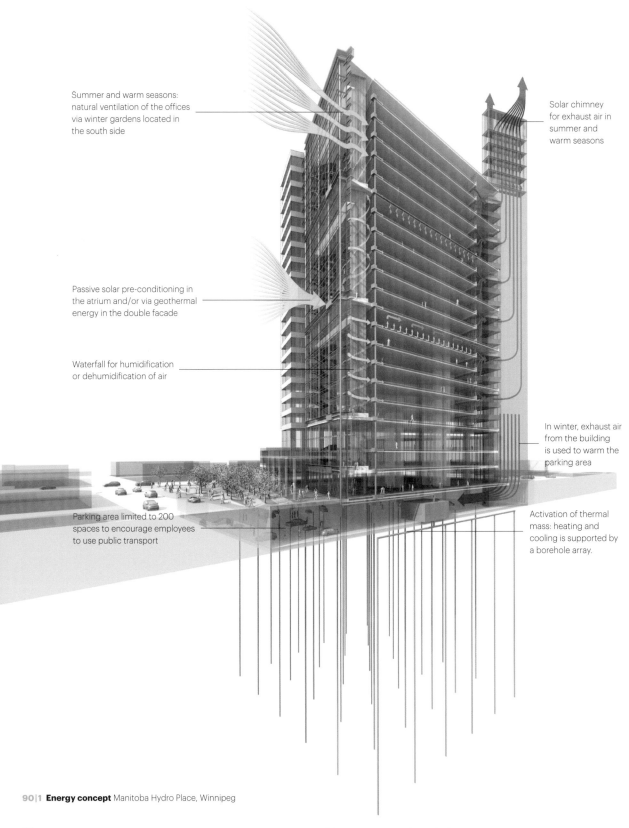

Summer and warm seasons: natural ventilation of the offices via winter gardens located in the south side

Solar chimney for exhaust air in summer and warm seasons

Passive solar pre-conditioning in the atrium and/or via geothermal energy in the double facade

Waterfall for humidification or dehumidification of air

In winter, exhaust air from the building is used to warm the parking area

Parking area limited to 200 spaces to encourage employees to use public transport

Activation of thermal mass: heating and cooling is supported by a borehole array.

90|1 **Energy concept** Manitoba Hydro Place, Winnipeg

this time more than 7000 students are registered at the university with its campus of 73 hectares and a view of the Mediterranean Sea – one of the last green spaces in the inner city of Beirut, also referred to as the 'Garden of Beirut'. The dense vegetation of the northern slope where the university is situated results in unique micro-climatic conditions on the campus. These permit natural ventilation driven by the cooler air descending to the lower regions of the campus.

The Charles Hostler Student Center includes a large sports and basket-ball hall, an indoor swimming pool, squash courts, an auditorium, offices, and a café. It is located directly on the Corniche of Beirut, with individual functions accommodated in separate buildings. The free spaces between these permit local winds to pass across the grounds. The ensemble profits from the constant movement of air through utilisation of seasonal wind conditions and the cycle of offshore and onshore winds, so that spaces between the buildings can cool off. They are oriented towards the sea and parallel to the slope, which means that the natural flow of air is not interrupted: the desired cooling effect can be achieved and the quality of indoor and outdoor air is improved.

The materials of the courtyard surfaces, corridors, and walls are selected according to visual and thermal requirements (91|1) – they absorb solar radiation, yet prevent glare. Sandstone walls offer thermal mass for radi-ant cooling during the day, and water walls using seawater support the micro-climate. The activation of thermal mass for cooling and heating is fed by a central supply system. Heat from the cooling systems is with-drawn exclusively via groundwater wells – due to infiltrating seawater here – with winter temperatures of 15 °C and summer temperatures of a maximum of 26 °C. Brackish water flows straight back to the Mediterra-nean. Therefore, operation of the system does not require a cooling tower, and no technical structures have to be placed on the building rooftops. Instead, the roofs of the auditorium, squash centre, and café are open to the public: they offer good views and collect rainwater that is stored in a cistern. Excellent indoor thermal comfort during the hot and humid summer months is achieved by means of radiative cooling and basic mechanical ventilation.

91|1 Charles Hostler Student Center, Beirut

Louvre Abu Dhabi, Abu Dhabi (UAE), in planning, Ateliers Jean -Nouvel The ruling council of the United Arab Emirates decided that Saadiyat Island off the coast of Abu Dhabi should become home to a cultural city with attractions including four museums and an arts com-plex. The special requirements of Abu Dhabi's hot and humid climate in summer have already been described in the section on the masterplan for Masdar City (» p. 87). The huge solar gains – the sun is almost in the zenith during the summer months – place high demands on shading and light filtration, features which have a long tradition in the history of Arab architecture. For example, in an oasis, the centre of life in a desert region,

92|1 and 92|2 Complex **light simulations** illustrate a 'rain of light' and light conditions beneath the dome. Louvre Abu Dhabi

palm trees always provide the first layer of shading and filtration, a shelter under which other plants can grow and outdoor life can take place. Ateliers Jean Nouvel was commissioned to design the Louvre Abu Dhabi in a location right next to the sea. Specifications call for a classic museum based on existing French museums like the Louvre, the Centre Pompidou, or the Musée Quai Branly. The design comprises an ensemble of impressive buildings on an artificial island with individual structures to accommodate the museum program. These are separated by generous places. One of the outstanding features is an extremely shallow dome with a diameter of 180 metres and covering the museum complex. The dome is elevated approximately 9 metres above street level and even cantilevers above the sea (92|1). Intricate perforations of the dome make it possible to limit the solar gains of the entire area. The architect envisages a 'rain of light', with patterns changing according to the sun's position (92|2). To make sure that the light spots are clearly defined, the size of each opening takes into account the effect of divergence, which results in a diffuse brightness, rather than an image of illumination, if openings are too small. Natural sources of cooling are used to create a pleasant micro-climate in the outdoor area beneath the dome. These include the earth, the sea, and radiative cooling at night, combined with cooling of the thermal mass of the ground and building walls. Museum visitors are supposed to be able to experience the space beneath the dome as a unique outdoor area, in sharp contrast to the brightness and heat beyond the roof-like projection.

Conclusion

The closer the connection between architecture and its specific location, and the better its comprehension of the genius loci as the starting point of planning is, the more sustainable the design of buildings can be.

Sustainability – an ideology initiated by a small group in central Europe some decades ago, is now ubiquitous: former American presidential candidate Al Gore received a Nobel Peace Prize for an alarming film and an information campaign on the state of our planet. Many celebrities all over the world become personally and financially involved in all sorts of environmental projects, concerned with issues ranging from saving the rain forest to biocosmetics. More and more products – fuel-saving cars, plant-based household cleaners, fair trade designer fashion made of organic cotton produced in a socially acceptable manner in Africa, organic fast food menus using only locally grown food products, briefcases manufactured from recycled tractor tire tubes, biodegradable slippers made of coconut fibre and natural latex in India – are advertised in terms of their environmental compatibility; ecological awareness and action are now an integral part of the corporate identity of many companies.

But how will this notion of sustainability continue into the future? Is it a wave, a trend like many others before – with the counter-movement just around the corner? However, one thing is for sure: the subjects that the neo-green movement has made aware of – climate change, overpopulation, shortage of resources, environmental pollution, species decline etc. – certainly are not trends, but facts. We should expect to deal with them in the future as well.

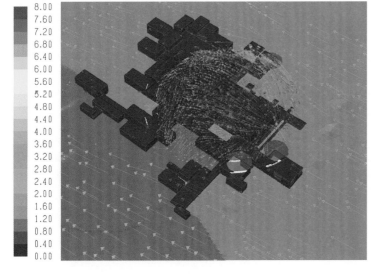

8.00
7.60
7.20
6.80
6.40
6.00
5.60
5.20
4.80
4.40
4.00
3.60
3.20
2.80
2.40
2.00
1.60
1.20
0.80
0.40
0.00

93|1 **Flow simulations** are used to control the dome's ventilation concept. Louvre Abu Dhabi

Common Sense Instead of High Tech

Text Jochen Paul, Jakob Schoof

About 40 percent of our energy consumption results from the construction and operation of buildings. Therefore, the energy efficiency and energy supply of buildings are of particular relevance in the discussion on climate change, security of supply, and reduction of energy consumption. Another important challenge is the creation of a pleasant indoor climate. Although we spend about 90 percent of our time in enclosed spaces, less than 30 percent of all buildings offer a healthy environment for their occupants, with air quality, indoor climate, and daylight exerting a major influence on their health, well-being, and performance.

New approaches to living and working

Since 2009 the largest manufacturer of roof window and skylight systems in the world, Velux, has been taking part in a pan-European experiment called 'Model Home 2020'. In this context, projects in five different countries have been carried out in an effort to develop new approaches to living and working in a pleasant indoor climate with a high rate of daylight intake and optimal energy efficiency. Six demonstration projects were designed that react to the various climatic and cultural conditions in the respective countries. The aim is to find solutions and strategies that can be used to create energy-efficient buildings with high user comfort in the future, as well as to gain knowledge on different energy-saving technologies. What all the Model Homes have in common is that they, as 'active houses', generate energy using renewable energy sources, and that they use this energy in a highly efficient manner, due to a complex control system for heating, ventilation, and shading. The qualitative and quantitative monitoring phase, in part lasting a number of years, offers the business sector important findings regarding the validity of theoretical propositions based on their practical application.

For questions on energy and handling resources cf. Parametric Design Systems » p. 52, Sustainable Urban Development » p. 72, 77, Understanding Buildings as Systems » p. 82–93, Building Processes of Tomorrow » p. 125, Collaboration of Industry and Research » p. 130, Research Initiative 'Future Building' » p. 136, 139ff.

94|1 Home for Life, Lystrup (DK) 2009, AART Architects

Two Danish concept houses were the first in line in 2009: the single-family house 'Home for Life' in Lystrup near Århus (94|1) and an administration building called 'Green Lighthouse' at the University of Copenhagen (95|1). The latter was also one of the exhibits at the UN Climate Conference in 2009. The monitoring phases of these two projects have been concluded. In 2010, they were followed by 'Sunlighthouse' in Pressbaum, west of Vienna (95|2) and 'Light Active House' in Hamburg. The final two projects began in 2011 and include 'CarbonLight Homes' in Rothwell, Great Britain and 'Maison Air et Lumière' in Verrières-le-Buisson, France.

The Model Homes were preceded by other demonstration projects such as 'SOLTAG' (2005) – a partially prefabricated modular house, designed to allow addition of a further story to flat roof buildings in moderate climate regions – as well as 'Atika' (2006) – a counterpart of SOLTAG for Mediterranean climate regions. Both were developed in collaboration with diverse partners from the building industry. The projects may differ in detail, but share a common starting point: the rather one-sided emphasis on energy saving in the climate discussion at that time. In contrast to this, the liveability aspect played a major role, in addition to the obligatory energy efficiency of the two houses.

LightActive House

The LightActive House in Hamburg-Wilhelmsburg is the German contribution to the Europe-wide 'Model Home 2020' experiment (95|3), and at the same time, the second realised sub-project of the IBA (International Building Exhibition) Hamburg. LightActive House is a modernised family home with a structure typical for housing developments dating back to the 1950s. It is located on a site covering an area of 1100 square metres and also includes a kitchen garden. The experiment is intended to demonstrate how optimal energy efficiency and a very high liveability rating can be combined within a demanding modernisation project. The aims include achievement of a net-zero-energy standard (including private power consumption), CO_2 neutrality of construction and operation, as well as a healthy indoor climate for the occupants, with plenty of daylight and fresh air.

The development of LightActive House was supervised by a competence team composed of experts in the fields of architecture and light planning. Within a closed competition at the Chair of Design and Energy-Efficient Building at the Technical University Darmstadt supervised by Prof. Manfred Hegger, new ideas, concepts, and models were proposed by students. The winning design '... home-grown' by Katharina Fey picks up the idea of self-sufficiency and independence and adapts it to the requirements of the 21st century: the 'produce' is comprised of energy and light, rather than vegetables. The design was devel-

95|1 Green Lighthouse, Copenhagen (DK) 2009, Christensen & Co Architects

95|2 Sunlighthouse, Pressbaum (A) 2010, Hein-Troy Architekten

95|3 LightActive House, Hamburg-Wilhelmsburg (D) 2010, Katharina Fey, Manfred Hegger, Ostermann Architekten

1

Hegger, Manfred et al.: 'Ökobilan-
zierung.' [Ecological Balance.] Velux
Model Home 2020. 'LightActive
House' Hamburg. Ecological balance
of the Velux Model Home in
Hamburg-Wilhelmsburg. Final Report.
Darmstadt 2011

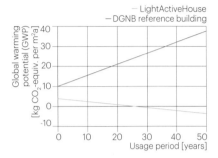

96|1 **Development of the global warming
potential (GWP)** of the LightActive House and a
DGNB reference building across 50 years. The
global warming potential due to construction and
energy demands is amortised by the PV power
fed to the network after 26 years.

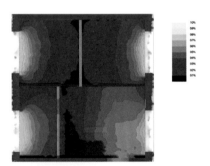

96|2 Daylight in rooms can be determined using
the **daylight factor**. This performance indicator
measures the percentage of daylight outdoors
reaching indoor space. LightActive House, Hamburg-Wilhelmsburg

oped further by Velux and TU Darmstadt in close collaboration with
specialist planners and the author of the design.

The objective of achieving a positive CO_2 balance over the entire life
cycle of the building turned out to be particularly challenging. This
means that all greenhouse gas emissions caused by manufacture of the
building materials are compensated during the usage period by avoiding
emissions through use of renewable energies. To prove this, a complete
ecological balance of the building was carried out at the Chair of Design
and Energy-Efficient Building at TU Darmstadt after completion of planning.[1] Every single building component was examined with regard to its
grey energy, CO_2 emissions, and a number of further environmental
effects. The decision to build the extension of the LightActive House
using only wood (except for the floor slab) was particularly advantageous
in this respect.

The ecological balance shows that in operation, LightActive House
avoids more CO_2 emissions than it causes through consumption of elec-
tricity for heating and hot water. In addition, even the CO_2 emissions
related to creation, maintenance, and disposal of the building construction are compensated after 26 years of operation. As result, the building
can be classified as 'CO_2 positive' from that date onwards (96|1).

The lighting design played a central role in the development of the Light-
Active House, which was based on extensive studies by light planner
Prof. Peter Andres. The results of daylight analyses were included in the
design process at an early stage, allowing optimal incorporation within
a dynamic integrated design process (96|2). The special focus on opti-
mised utilisation of daylight makes it possible to achieve a high liveability rating as well as good energy efficiency, thanks to solar gains enabled
by the building's windows. Furthermore, plenty of daylight and generous
views allow occupants to perceive nature's daily and annual rhythms.

Monitoring: questions and methods

After completion of modernisation and conversion work, a family will
live in the LightActive House for a period of two years from late 2011
onward in order to test 'future living'. This test phase is a central component of the project, as it is important to the company to find out how
this vision of plenty of daylight, fresh air, and outdoor views fares in
practice. Energy consumption and indoor climate will be measured
constantly during the two-year period, and the members of the family
living in the LightActive House are also required to document their
experience of living in the house. The aim is to find out more specific
information on the design of an environmentally compatible housing
solution capable of offering residents a healthy indoor climate and great
liveability This is based on the conviction that, for sustainable housing
to meet future needs, the focus has to be on human beings. They are,

after all, a building's users. A house should be adapted to suit the requirements of the inhabitants, and not the other way round.

Prof. Peter Andres from the Peter Behrens School of Architecture in Düsseldorf considers the connection between daylight intake and how the family actually deals with daylight as the central issue. Daylight intake varies according to annual seasons as well as during the course of a day. The extent to which the quantity of light specified by DIN 5053 is adequate for living spaces is also to be investigated.

The aim of Prof. Bernd Wegener, a specialist in social research at the Humboldt University Berlin who is also involved in the monitoring, is to develop instruments for measuring perceived quality of living conditions, living comfort, and subjective habitability indicators. This serves as basis for a survey on the subject of 'Living and Environmental Awareness' to be conducted with the general public after the two-year research and measurement period.

Before the monitoring, suitable measurement methods have to be specified and questionnaires and interview designs have to be developed and approved – always keeping in mind the question of how much individuality and self-determination is necessary to feel 'at home' and for the family to identify itself with the new housing situation, so as to keep distortion of the monitoring results to a minimum. The family's housing situation prior to moving into the house also has to be recorded, in order to be able to conduct a valid comparison afterwards.

Active House

The insights and findings gained from these diverse demonstration objects and research projects are accessible on a manufacturer-independent platform titled 'Active House'.[2] It offers the building industry an opportunity for exchange in the field of sustainable construction and buildings of the future.

The Active House is concerned with three key subjects: energy, indoor climate, and environment (97|2). Therefore, an Active House not only offers a positive contribution to the energy balance of a building, but also towards healthier and more comfortable living conditions for its inhabitants, as well as facilitating positive interaction with the environment: this is the central thesis. The aim is to achieve a successful balance of the three above-mentioned aspects – a holistic approach that is also found in the detailed specifications for Active Houses as developed by the platform.[3]

Approximately 30 experts from different European universities, research institutes, and building product manufacturers were involved in the development process, including the Technical University of Denmark, the Universities of Århus, Darmstadt, Eindhoven, Porto and Bucharest, the Danish Building Research Institute, the International Initiative for a Sustainable Built Environment (iiSBE), and an insulation material manufacturer.

97|1 Modernised top floor of a typical 1950s family house, **LightActive House**, Hamburg-Wilhelmsburg (D) 2010, Katharina Fey, Manfred Hegger, Ostermann Architekten

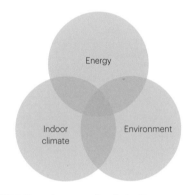

97|2 **Central aspects of an Active House**

2

http://activehouse.info (accessed on 02.11.2011)

3

http://activehouse.info/about-active-house/specification (accessed on 02.11.2011)

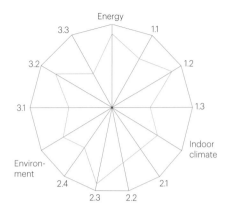

On the one hand, the Active House specifications are intended as a planning aid for sustainable buildings – especially smaller residential buildings – and as a catalogue of criteria for assessment of their sustainability on the other hand. The three main categories are divided into ten sub-categories, each of which is evaluated in terms of qualitative and quantitative parameters (98|1). The experts intentionally refrained from a purely quantitative evaluation, because certain building characteristics – such as the quality of views to the exterior or the possibility of individual regulation of indoor climate by the user – cannot be expressed in numbers.

Stance and conviction

Like most companies in the sector, Velux also perceives itself as a supplier of systems and solutions. These should not only be as simple as possible to use, but also only as complex and technical as absolutely necessary. Per Arnold Andersen, head of the Daylight, Energy and Indoor Climate Department, calls these 'no nonsense solutions'. He believes that apartments and houses should be as easy to use as possible. A lot can be learned from history regarding adaptation to the respective climate through the orientation of buildings, the function of individual rooms, the size and position of windows, depth of roof overhang, window shutters and curtains, etc. Inventing things from scratch is not really required – all the products needed to fulfil the EU specifications for 2020 are basically already available. However, what is essential is to observe how the individual components of a building interact and to employ the existing products appropriately.

This is also confirmed by Strategic Project Manager Lone Feifer, who emphasises that Velux is and intends to remain a manufacturer of roof windows. The aim is certainly not to encroach on the territory of their partners in the building industry. However, the company does maintain a perspective and offers a product that plays an important role for the sustainability of architecture. She states that Active House is intended to initiate a discussion on the qualities of the product.

According to the founder of the company, Villum Kann Rasmussen, "One experiment is better than a thousand expert views." This is another reason why Model Homes 2020 resulted in many new products, new technologies, and diverse prototypes, either novel as such or in their combination. The primary aim is to gain knowledge from implementation of theories in practice, and to feed this information back to science in order to obtain new findings – and improved theories. According to Lone Feifer, experiences to date have clearly shown that it will be possible to make Active Houses a customary standard by 2020. A careful coordination of technology, building materials, architectural concept, and living requirements as individual components is of primary importance in this context.

Velux intends to make the findings derived from planning of the LightActive House and development of the Active House specifications accessible to a broader public audience. As a member of the German Sustainable Building Council (DGNB), the company is actively involved in a working group that is developing a new occupancy profile for smaller residential buildings within the DGNB system. This will make building certification, previously restricted to larger investment projects, more readily available to everyday building projects.

Knowledge exchange

As a supplier of roof windows and skylights, Velux is obviously interested in how high-quality daylight can be directed inside buildings – but also what light intensities correspond to our visual and biological requirements, since the biorhythm of the human organism requires a range of different degrees of brightness during the course of a day.

Moreover, the Daylight, Energy and Indoor Climate Department of the company works with anthropologists who conduct research on topics including how particular practices, e.g. ventilating a room in the morning or the desire to smell good could be of significance to the subject of building ventilation. Other topics include the effects of daylight, natural ventilation, and the quality of air and light on the treatment of illnesses such as asthma or depression. In this regard, the interface between medical research and the field of architecture and building is of particular interest: Per Arnold Andersen feels that the two professions don't interact as often as they should. He states that this may explain why it takes so long for the knowledge of one discipline to reach the other.

To intensify this exchange, Velux has been holding a Daylight Symposium every two years since 2005. It is an opportunity for top researchers to meet and get an idea of what new findings in their fields are of significance to the activities of the company. This considerably shortens the time required for the findings of a particular discipline to impact interdisciplinary research.

The subject of the symposium in 2013 is 'Daylight in the Perspective of Existing Building Stock'. According to the German Federal Statistical Office, about half of the 39 million housing units in Germany are between 30 and 60 years old and in need of energy efficiency modernisation. This represents an enormous potential for energy saving and climate protection. The monitoring of the LightActive House in Hamburg is of particular interest in this context: rather than a new construction, the project purposely dealt with renovation of existing building stock to be realised on a modular basis.

99|1 Living/dining area, **Home for Life**, Lystrup (DK) 2009, AART Architects

For the potential of use changes and renovations cf. Back to Being Social » *p. 61f*, *Sustainable Urban Development* » *p. 73*, *Understanding Buildings as Systems* » *p. 84*, *Building Processes of Tomorrow* » *p. 127*, *Research Initiative 'Future Building'* » *p. 137*

Trend Predictions – Approaches, Methods, Opportunities

Text Markus Schlegel, Sabine Foraita

In principle, urban planners, architects and designers work towards the near future. Among the issues that constantly drive these creative professions are people's future needs and requirements. These issues further include the search for design solutions ranging between the existing and the new, but also viable from both an urban development aspect and the point of view of clients or architects. Every design basically represents a thesis on how to deal with built space and the physical environment in the future and how this can express itself in formal-aesthetic terms. But how to create a basis for design development? How can designers and architects employ methods of future studies?

A combination of methods has been developed at the Institute of International Trendscouting (IIT) at the University of Applied Sciences and Arts (HAWK) in Hildesheim, which allows future design scenarios to be determined in terms of colour, shape, material, and context. To achieve this, criteria are defined with regard to content, as well as visual representation of scenarios, so that basic developments can be described as clearly as necessary, but as freely interpretable as possible.

Observing the past in a cultural context

Making a statement on the development of design in the future requires, on the one hand, an analysis of formal-aesthetic developments in the past, and on the other hand, determining the factors that influence design, in order to draw relevant conclusions for the future.

A research project conducted at the IIT began with specifying the factors that influence design according to nature, ideology, politics, economy, technology, and art during various decades, followed by a study of their significance, and eventually their visualisation.

Art, design, and architecture are always a particular expression of a specific attitude towards life and a cultural stance, which is inherent in the objects and structures created. The explanation at the UNESCO World Conference in Mexico City in 1982 states "that in its widest sense, culture may now be said to be the whole complex of distinctive spiritual, material, intellectual and emotional features that characterise a society or social group. It includes not only the arts and letters, but also modes of life, the fundamental rights of the human being, value systems, traditions and beliefs."[1] A particularly important cultural factor is not included in this list, even though it describes the major part of our daily life: the artefacts and media that surround us and significantly influence our habits of viewing and acting. Therefore, they also represent a kind of 'sign system' that has a significant influence on our current and future life.

We live in a time with considerable interaction between inside and outside – between private and public life. This is why architecture, interior spaces, and articles of daily use mirror different needs, general customs, and viewing habits. The media also have a powerful influence on our perception modes and viewing habits. In the so-called information and knowledge society, they have a sustained effect on our daily life – and therefore, also on design.

Our research project involved classification of formal-aesthetic forms of expression of architecture, design, art, and fashion according to year, which allows identification of direct relations, as well as time-delayed influences. The studies were initially limited to German-speaking regions, but there are plans to include all of Europe in a further step.

The state of the respective society is directly connected to the factors of influence. It seeks and finds its expression in design. A specific style, which can be described as a concentration of signs, is the formal-aesthetic mirror image (or reflection) of social sentiment. For example, the 1960s and 1970s were characterised by a dominant youth culture and a belief in technological progress. The signs or codes that correspond to a society are expressed in shapes, colours, materials, and patterns. Most people are able to correlate the patterns and colours of the 1960s and 1970s to these decades (103|1). They are clear signs of the ethos of this period and evident in various areas such as architecture, design, and

1

Mexico City Declaration on Cultural Policies. World Conference on Cultural Policies, Mexico City, 06 August 1982.
http://portal.unesco.org/culture/en/ev.php-URL_ID=12762&URL_DO=DO_TOPIC&URL_SECTION=201.html (accessed on 30.04.2012)

fashion, which mutually enrich each other. An accumulation of formal manifestations of a sign character can lead to the establishment of significances, and hence to the development of a trend or even a style.

The attitude of society normally has a particularly pronounced influence on design in times impacted by crises. The influence of the already virulent topic of sustainability has increased yet again after the catastrophe in Fukushima – which also has an effect on architecture and design. Such crises have a worldwide influence on the attitude of a society. However, as so-called wild cards of future studies, they evade prediction.

The available technological options also have a considerable influence on design. New materials, as well as manufacturing and processing methods strongly impact formal-aesthetic attributes. For example, the use of plastics offered revolutionary design opportunities, permitting a completely new vocabulary of forms.

An analysis of the past six decades, on the one hand, indicates a development towards globalisation, while a trend towards increasing individualisation was identified within the past three decades. This leads to a diversification of trends, also promoted by technological development and the associated design freedom, and accompanied by increasing self-fulfilment. Another fact identified in the research project was that there wasn't only one dominant trend in each phase. Instead, there were trends existing in parallel, secondary trends, and counter-trends of various kinds.

Observing the past in terms of design and architecture

What role do colour and surface play in the architecture of the 20th and 21st century? What differences in the observation and effect of solitary buildings, designed urban or spatial ensembles, as well as interior spaces can be identified?

First of all, it should be noted that the importance of symbolic architecture and interior design for prestige buildings or brand architecture has been increasing since the beginning of the 21st century. This is often characterised by an innovative architectural language, which frequently permits a development of new formal solutions by utilisation of new materials and technologies, such as digital tools. This way, a subtle to radical departure from our previously established viewing habits occurs, together with an extension of our cultural memory through new 'visual components'. While the function of symbolic structures such as the Centre Pompidou in Paris (1977) still plays a dominant role by turning the inside of the architecture outwards in sculptural terms, within the last ten years 'form follows function' as code of honour has become increasingly less important. Even the seemingly inviolable rules of architectural design formulated by Adolf Loos in his 'Ornament and Crime' from 1908,

For further aspects of social and societal change cf. Back to Being Social » *p. 60, 69, Sustainable Urban Development* » *p. 71f., Living Ergonomics* » *p. 123, Research Initiative 'Future Building'* » *p. 137*

Trend Predictions – Approaches, Methods, Opportunities

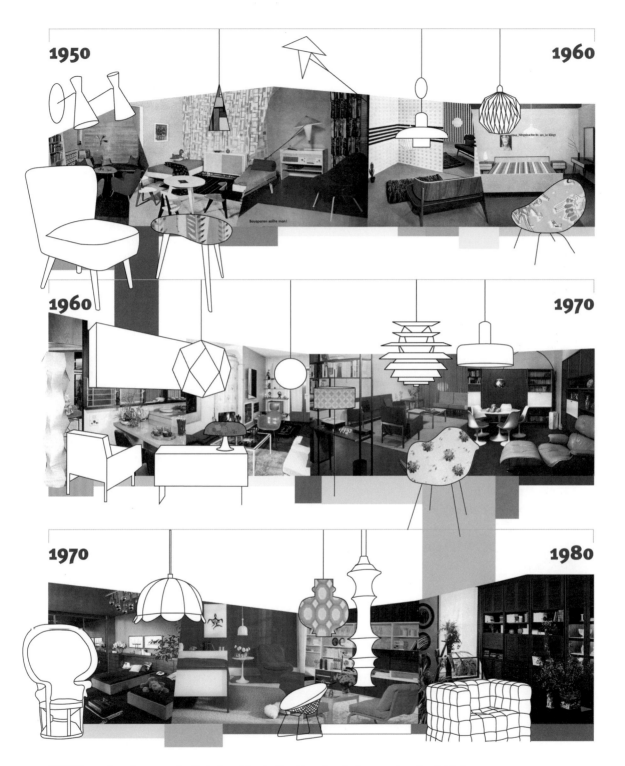

103|1 The **roadmap** is an exemplary illustration of the significant formal-aesthetic parameters of spatial design in the years 1950–1980. It visualises the course of previous trends and typical time-related colour profiles of interior design in Germany.

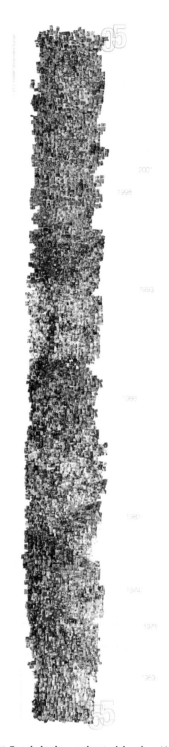

104|1 Epochal colour and material cycles with colour phases from 1955–2005

adopted by generations of students, appear to be less and less pertinent. The exclusive applicability of these two 'guidelines' of architectural language has receded since the turn of the century or even earlier. This has opened the gates for innovations and things previously unknown and encourages a new understanding of architecture and urban space.

We consider this to be a reason that warrants an intensive study of epochal developments in design, colour and form, especially in interior design since the 1950s: the multi-faceted, differentiated, and often also immensely time- and style-related design languages that merely found application in interior design, yet now also appear in architecture or in urban space, are becoming increasingly fast, direct, and uncomplicated. As mentioned earlier, for trend researchers to create models of the future, an analytical consideration of past epochs and the recent past is required as a basis (consideration of cycles). Our focus is on the past 60 years, during which a rapid development and change in the function, form, colour, and material of architecture, interior design, and design in general has occurred, driven by social requirements and technological advances.

The first part of our ColourSpaceColour ('FarbRaumFarbe') study focusses on interior space, patterns, structures, colours, and forms, while the second part deals with architecture and materiality. With the help of so-called observation models criteria for image sources and image selection in print and non-print media are defined, followed by identification and visualisation of the principles of change and the factors of influence on design processes in the past (105|1). These observation models were specifically developed by the IIT for filtration and representation of design-relevant significances by using a systematic analytical procedure. Data acquisition and analysis is carried out by staff trained in viewing tasks and sensitised with regard to design.

Individual colour and material typologies that emerged from trends and can be represented in a differentiated manner are described as epochal architecture, product, colour, and material profiles and documented in colour spectra (106|1 and 107|1). A roadmap is used for graphic illustration of developments. This is a chronological visualisation of all data of the study, comprising approximately 10,000 images, recorded in German-speaking regions between 1955 and 2010, and documented as relevant on the basis of significant image characteristics (104|1).

The past 60 years can be summarised in pastel, brown, brightening, colourful, or white phases. These phases can be illustrated as a colour-based progression independent of social or technical influences, which allows complex stylistic interpretations within a specific colour phase. This means that trends and secondary trends in comparable and type-related colour typologies exist in several design directions. In particular, different formal-aesthetic design preferences in varying milieus – depending on financial means and design affinity – can be determined, which is related to the development of an increasingly differentiated and globalised society from the 1950s onward.

It is significant that clear dominances of superordinate, theme-independent colour manifestations and typical colourations can be identified in the individual phases. This means that comparable time-related colour profiles can often be recognised in different stylistic or formal-aesthetic fields.

However, the ColourSpaceColour ('FarbRaumFarbe') study not only shows the change of specific epochal colour phases, but also the emergence of typical, recurrent colour combinations in the past 60 years. In parallel, formal developments of product design can be interpreted as semantic additions within a spatial context. Change phenomena, such as ornamental and non-ornamental, arising out of creative protest movements and attitudes of saturation also occur here. The collective desire to change applies to all elements of design.

The interaction of colour, pattern, material, and form, as well as social and technological development is obvious. For example, the brown phase that appeared in the middle of the 1970s – a change result from an extensive colourful phase from 1960 to about 1975 – developed at the same time as the worldwide oil crisis. 'Natural instead of plastic' is one of the slogans of materiality. Natural earth, sand, green, and wooden shades are in the foreground. The material and colour profile is additionally characterised by ethnologically and socially related influences from South and Central America. At this point we presume that this colour phase would have also occurred irrespective of social and ecological discussions. However, it is very likely that the above mentioned visually suitable and ethically logical materials would not have been used to the same extent, because social framework conditions certainly do influence the duration of a trend. The fact that this phase initiated the ongoing sustainability discussion that currently and once more is clearly expressed in the form, material, and colour vocabulary, evaded prior recognition.

What are trends?

The etymological meaning of the word trend suggests a process, tendency, and direction of movement or development. Two different interpretations of the term exist: classical and modern.

The classical interpretation describes trends as individual and social tendencies of development that directly or indirectly impact us sooner or later. According to the classical interpretation, trends are not to be confused with fads or zeitgeist-related currents. In this context, trends are described as slow-moving rather than fast-moving. This definition is equivalent to the etymological perspective, and therefore is also used in statistics.

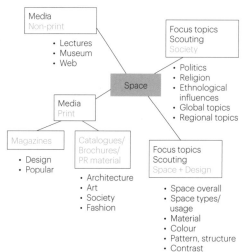

105|1 Mind map for scouting and observation space of formal-aesthetic developments and changes

"Wooden elements consistently appeared in the area of furniture and interior design in the years 1955-2010, differing only in the type of wood and the respective market penetration. Light and dark types of wood alternated in the degree of acceptance by the masses. This was dependent on social trends such as the change in ecological awareness of the 1970s, or the technical advance of plastic in the 1960s."

Translation of a quotation by Livia Baum, IIT HAWK Hildesheim, 2011

For parameters, methods and application examples of trend research cf. Sustainable Urban Development » *p. 75, Building Processes of Tomorrow* » *p. 125, Collaboration of Industry and Research* » *p. 130*

COLOUR | MATERIAL | SPACE |

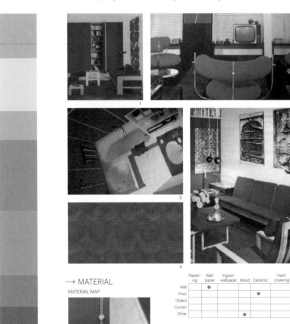

→ COLOUR |IMPRESSION|

light		dark
warm		cold
monotonous		rich in contrast
greyed		brilliant

→ COLOURATION

yellow		yellow-orange
orange		red-orange
red		red-violet
violet		blue-violet
blue		blue-green
green		green-yellow
white		black

→ COLOUR |WALL|

yellow		yellow-orange
orange		red-orange
red		red-violet
violet		blue-violet
blue		blue-green
green		green-yellow
white		black

→ COLOUR |FLOOR|

yellow		yellow-orange
orange		red-orange
red		red-violet
violet		blue-violet
blue		blue-green
green		green-yellow
white		black

→ COLOUR |OBJECT|

yellow		yellow-orange
orange		red-orange
red		red-violet
violet		blue-violet
blue		blue-green
green		green-yellow
white		black

COLOUR MAP

→ IMAGE

| avant-garde | | standard |
| staged | | common-place |

→ PATTERN

round		angular
organic		geometrical
small-sized		large-area
fancy		austere

PATTERN MAP

→ MATERIAL

MATERIAL MAP

	Plaster-ing	Wall-paper	Ingrain wallpaper	Wood	Ceramic	Hard covering	Laminate
Wall							
Floor							
Object							
Curtain							
Other							

	Ceramic	Stone	Glass	Steel	Synthetic	Textiles	Carpet
Wall							
Floor							
Object							
Curtain							
Other							

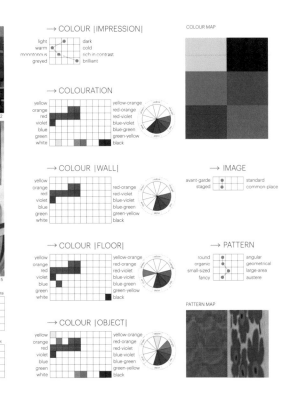

COLOUR SHADE | ORDER | CODING |

→ LCH

→ NCS

→ COLOUR-CODING ACCORDING TO LCH AND NCS

SIGNIFICANT COLOUR COMBINATIONS

→ COLOUR COMBINATION |SPACE|

→ COLOUR COMBINATION |OBJECT/SURFACE|

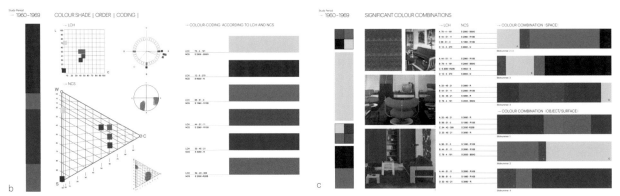

Observation models

a Colour/Material/Order
b Colour shade/Order/Coding
c Significant colour combinations

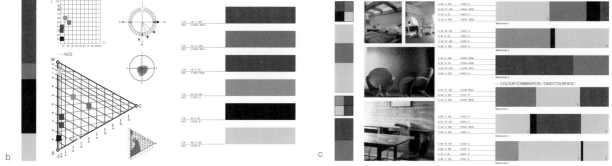

106–107|1 The **observation model** systematically queries the formal-aesthetic parameters in a room. Design-relevant positions can be identified and documented in a matrix with the help of methodical screening. Materiality, patterns, and formal relations are recorded and colour profiles are noted in the Natural Colour System (NCS) and the LCH colour space. Image observation models record image data in several waves, analyse, and evaluate them, in order to identify colour phases in the different epochs. When looking at the past, the observation models serve to formulate typical epochal colour phases. When looking at the present, they form a basis for trend monitoring and for scenario-like progressions of new colour profiles.

2

Opaschowski, Horst: Germany 2020. 'Wie wir morgen leben – Prognosen der Wissenschaft.' [How We Will Live Tomorrow – Scientific Forecasts] Wiesbaden 2006, p. 61f.

Colloquial use corresponds more to the modern interpretation of trend, which is based on a value pyramid, according to the future researcher Horst Opaschowski. Its peak is represented by a trend: an occurrence of medium or short duration.[2]

The IIT considers trends to be shifts in values with considerable intrinsic dynamics that are tangible and can be localised in many areas. Links between elementary reference objects are also described as trends. For example, these may involve new associative links that can be influenced by creative cells (i.e. segment areas or cooperation within the creative industry field) or can be promoted by the industry – but only under the condition that they can be integrated in already existing consumer perception patterns.

Trend research

Trend monitoring as a visual evaluation and documentation of trend scouting can act as a mirror of current tendencies and upcoming developments, yet also serve as a navigation and decision-making aid for industry or trade. Trend research at the IIT involves analysis and strategic study of an enormous flood of information from the areas of architecture and design, and separation of viable and design-relevant issues from unimportant and trivial matter. Using various perception models, such as the system perception map (» p. 112, 110 | 1) and further procedural steps, change processes are observed and reflected, but also generated on the basis of new linkages that are associative and design-related. Three types of trend monitoring are primarily created in the process:

- **Type 1:** General colour and material profiles represented by topical superordination and polar differentiation, yet very open and flexible as spectra. These can easily be transferred to different areas of application.
- **Type 2:** Polar, theme-related colour, material, and object moods (image clusters) that sketch the significant recordable basic characters of a specific trend direction. In a superordinate colour profile, these show possible semantic additions, such as patterns, structures, or shapes of the design or product world usually expressed as diverse stylistic interpretations (109 | 1).
- **Type 3:** Style and milieu worlds contoured according to polar colour profiles and stylistic parameters, thus addressing a clear target group. These are positioned very 'sharply', purposely minimising the scope of interpretation of the particular observer. This is intended to result in a clear and unambiguously customised image of the near future (109 | 2).

Trend monitoring for design developments and recommendations should not overwhelm the restrictions or viewing habits of observers. This is necessary to ensure correct decoding and appropriate classification, application, or acceptance of further design developments. This forms the basis for a broad approval or the beginning of an adaptation of a new formal idea. Design-related or formal new developments are always based on previous design languages or trends and are as such updates, modifications, or counter-programmes of existing sign systems. The designer always needs to take into account that the degree of ability to decode these varies within multi-layered cultural target groups – ranging from experts to laypeople.

If construction is carried out for heterogeneous user groups, for example a change in urban landscape through architecture, what needs to be taken into account is that the result will be evaluated by an entire society. In addition, the built structure should ideally be comprehensible without further explanation. Only in this case is acceptance likely. On the other hand, if spatial programmes are developed for design experts, i.e. the 'leitmilieu' of those with an affinity towards design, then the degree of progression can diverge more strongly from viewing habits. Subsequent medial transportation of the creation forms a basis for further adaptation towards individuals with less design affinity.

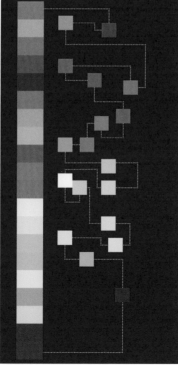

109|1 **Trend Monitoring Type 2**: Trend monitoring as a clustered colour profile of a specific epoch of 2006, which is topically delimited and described using semantic additions (images).

109|2 **Trend Monitoring Type 3**: Polar 'sharply positioned' colour profile of 2006 without semantic additions, i.e. not yet limited and defined as a style and milieu subject. The next step would be the selection of a suitable image for formal and material-related criteria.

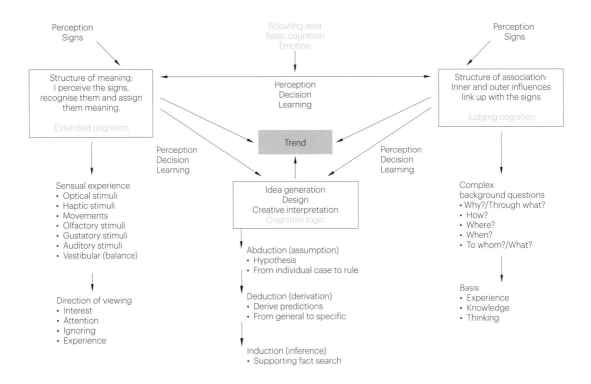

110|1 System perception map: The scouting procedure for change processes or new manifestations in architecture and design is organised by the observation, recognition, and inclusion of signs. Through application of cognitive logic, the combined interaction of basic cognition, extended cognition, and judging cognition leads to new interpretations and ideas.

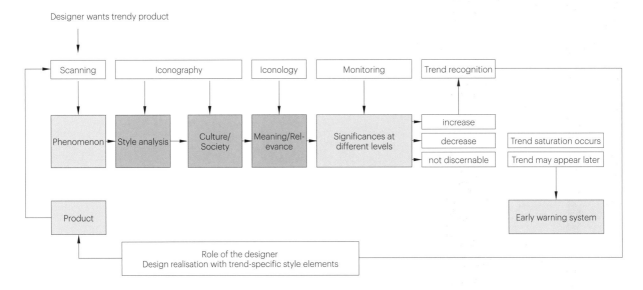

110|2 Schematic representation of a design process with trend-specific style elements: Trend-specific designs require constant thematic examination, observation, and creative conditioning. Statements on design-related significances can be made via classical space or image analysis and interpretation.

Yellow-Orange-
Red-Pink 2000–2006

2003–2006

Blue-Green

Black-White-
Silver-Grey

2006–2010

111|1 The three **distinctive colour phases of the years 2000–2010**: Significant colour and material profiles are determined and formulated using image observation models. The colour and material 'clouds' show colourations partly existing in parallel that can be perceived as dominant in each case.

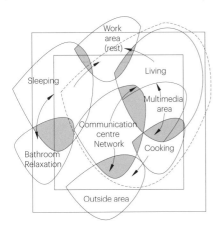

112|1 Floor plan development for the subject 'Future Living': Result of an expert survey in the year 2011

"Anyone who wants to look into the future or try to predict the future should know as much as possible about the present and the past."

Translation of a quotation by Opaschowski, Horst: 'Zukunft neu denken.' [New Future Thinking.] In: Popp, Reinhold; Schüll, Elmar: 'Zukunftsforschung und Zukunftsgestaltung.' [Future Studies and Future Design.] Berlin/Heidelberg 2009, p. 17

3
Buether, Axel: 'Die Bildung der räumlich-visuellen Kompetenz.' [Development of Spatio-Visual Competence.] Burg Giebichenstein 2010

The question on the specific design innovations demanded by society will continue to gain importance for businesses, but also for architects and designers. For example, controversial discussions on the topics of colouration, materiality, and form in architecture have been conducted for many decades. Currently, these subjects are once more becoming the focus of attention within many design processes. As part of cityscape development, colouration turns into a marketing factor, while architecture becomes a product, and the design scope of built envelopes increases through material innovations. There is an obligation and urgency to act strategically with regard to future-relevant aesthetic developments. The scope ranges from particular progressions of existing sustainable developments to the creation of digital models with capacity of initiating thought-provoking impulses or further development of viewing habits. As result, a certain degree of innovation pressure is promoted.

The specific subject of colour or colouration is only one parameter in this regard, but its influence should not be underestimated. Trend colours are a symbolic expression of differing prevailing orientations that primarily serve to demonstrate affiliation to an idealised user group and to represent the 'zeitgeist'. As part of a marketing concept, they may also aim to generate a difference in meaning. In the interaction with other formal-aesthetic parameters, trend colours represent the associated visually perceptible sign system, in relation to trend monitoring types 1–3. Therefore, specific colour profiles, such as for ecology and sustainability as higher-order topics, can be identified to a varying extent in all three monitoring types. However, the formal-aesthetic parameters determined, created, and formulated for the respective type-specific monitorings vary in terms of their characteristics and their subsequent target group orientation.

But how do perception and sign systems function, and how are the correct trends and codes identified? The direct connection between perception and sign interpretation, as well as how the field of trend and future research deals with them, is described as a cycle and interaction network on four levels of cognition by using a system perception map (110|1). The use of this method scheme, which is based on findings in the fields of neurobiology and cognitive psychology of the 'Development of Spatiovisual Competence' ('Bildung der räumlich-visuellen Kompetenz')[3] and the method set of the IIT, is intended to demonstrate interconnections and processes of trend scouting and monitoring. The system perception map describes perception criteria and mechanisms, the position of the decoding of perceived structures of meaning and association within the overall process, as well as the creative interpretation of the cognition logic of a subject.

The identification of change processes or new manifestations in architecture and design basically functions through observation, recognition, and inclusion of signs. Basic and extended cognition play a decisive role here. Basic cognition is the interaction between fundamentally existing knowledge on the subject and the basic knowledge of reality, bound to emotions. This way, the information that the brain receives forms the basis for an understanding of the observation area that surrounds us. Extended cognition describes the inclusion of signs and codes as the actual trend scouting. The acquired data are allocated to a specific structure of meaning through decoding. This process is a multi-step 'distillation process' in which we repeatedly analyse, sort, and topically assign the gathered data according to our observation models. As opposed to the emotionally based 'unconscious knowledge' of basic cognition, extended cognition is based on signs that can be acknowledged and learnt, on methodology and process flow, as well as on conditioning by experts.

Judging cognition as a further interpretation of the respective structure of meaning eventually forms the association level. This is where image and information material is questioned, analysed, reallocated, and summarised in polar formal-aesthetic groups, according to further criteria, such as viability or the occurrence of a phenomenon in the past. In the resulting cognition logic, a trend monitoring capable of clearly describing and representing formal-aesthetic criteria can be generated as a derivation using justifiable assumptions and empirical values.

Future studies

Which specific methods are appropriate for future studies in the area of design, and why should designers and architects deal with these? The scientific observation of housing as a basic requirement and as one particular topic central to human beings is regarded as very important by our faculty. In this regard, our work methods reflect the increasingly interdisciplinary work flows of the creative industry and the current economic reality.

We can use objects to interpret the past and create an image of it. Why shouldn't this also work for the future? The analytical consideration of the past and present using our observation models and the methodically determined images of the future based on these, which we call trend monitoring, help us to classify and formulate developments and enrich these with the corresponding background information, allowing us to carry out ongoing and in-depth future studies.

If the advancement of future studies leads to its shifting from a prognostic towards a scenario-based way of illustrating future developments,[4] then urban planners, architects, and designers are uniquely suited to create future scenarios. They always work with images of future mindsets and practices. Their work as such is future-oriented and strives to pro-

"Therefore, this means that a person recognises something that has changed or that forms an unusual, new phenomenon and focusses on it, by taking it to pieces, analysing backgrounds, looking for similar phenomena, and putting these pieces back together again."

Translation of a quotation by Livia Baum, IIT HAWK Hildesheim, 2011

4

Grunwald, Armin: 'Wovon ist die Zukunftsforschung eine Wissenschaft.' [What is the Underlying Science of Future Studies.] In: ibid., p. 26

"Looking ahead means to make aware, to provoke questions, to invite answers, to encourage to act, to develop solutions and strategies, as well as to take measures."

Translation of a quotation by Opaschowski, Horst: 'Zukunft neu denken.' [New Future Thinking.] In: Popp, Reinhold; Schüll, Elmar: 'Zukunftsforschung und Zukunftsgestaltung.' [Future Studies and Future Design.] Berlin/Heidelberg 2009, p. 19

Intelligent or smart materials *are materials that have properties that can be switched on electrically or magnetically. They are particularly useful when they are employed to simplify complicated technical systems or achieve completely new functions and characteristics.*

cf: http://www.isc.fraunhofer.de/ newsdetails0+M5df20eb004e.html (accessed on 20.10.2011)

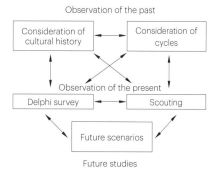

114|1 Canon of Methods for Future Studies.
The individual research levels on the observation of the past and the present form the basis for formulating future scenarios.

ject requirements and possibilities of future utilisation into the design process. However, this requires sound information on possible models of living and topics that will eventually become more important. This type of information can be obtained by conducting expert surveys and expert discussions in the form of Delphi surveys. A Delphi survey is carried out in several rounds that build up on each other, in which the results of earlier rounds are confirmed, detailed, and developed further. Targeted questionnaire design is used to encourage experts to develop solutions for future ways of living. The combination of an observation of cycles, trend scouting, monitoring, and Delphi surveys forms the basis of the creation of future scenarios at the ITT.

For instance, observation of cycles has revealed an increase in individualisation, which is expressed in personal action and requires corresponding design solutions. This affects ways of life and related scenarios, such as of housing. One future way of life recognised and confirmed in an expert survey was the patchwork family. Meshing areas for living and working, for sleep and wellness, or intentions of consciously living a healthy life and to relax are central aspects of current spatial requirements (112|1). An increasingly intelligent and interactive integration of media in living spaces as well as vertical and horizontal surfaces, integrated in familiar components that act as spatial perimeter, is unstoppable. In addition, a development towards linking interior and exterior areas of living space is desired by the experts who participated in the survey and is already in demand, at least within certain strata of society. This is also reflected in the use of materials that experts expect to be employed both for interior and exterior spaces. Therefore, the use of smart materials, as well as materials that contribute to a particular atmosphere will play an important role.

Conclusion

On the basis of the method set employed at the Institute of International Trendscouting, three types of scenario development can be identified: Type 1 is a descriptive scenario that allows a broad scope of interpretation with regard to formal-aesthetic criteria. This form of description is used for preliminary decision or further discussion with experts. Type 2 is a descriptive and visual scenario in which text and image messages are coordinated so that the corresponding text elements complement the abstract images of the future. The observer is necessitated to close the gaps in the picture, which allows a personal, yet directed view. This form of scenario representation is the one most commonly used for design and innovation processes at the IIT. The scenario contents are primarily related to architecture, interior design, and design. Type 3 is a purely pictorial scenario that typically describes a subject or design typology in the form of a kind of 'mood graphic'; it can trigger impulses or discussions and developments.

The philosopher Karl Raimund Popper held the opinion that only audacious theories could advance science.[5] Applying this to design professions would mean that we must have visionary designs as reference objects to advance future design. If we don't want science fiction films to be the decisive factor that influences our concept of the future, and if we want to develop our viewing habits further in an active and professional manner, then it will become increasingly necessary to determine and create such desirable and tangible scenarios. This observation is valid for the field of architecture and design, as well as the economic and higher education reality. Our aim at HAWK is to develop this issue further, together with our network of partners and in dialogue with designers, the industry, and experts active in diverse fields of work. _____

5

Popper, Karl Raimund: 'Das Abgrenzungsproblem.' [The Demarcation Problem.] In: Mill, David (ed.): 'Lesebuch. Ausgewählte Texte zur Erkenntnistheorie, Philosophie der Naturwissenschaften, Metaphysik, Sozialphilosophie.' [Reader. Selected Texts on the Theory of Cognition, Philosophy of the Natural Sciences, Metaphysics, Social Philosophy. Tübingen 1995, p. 107]

116|1 **Ørestad College**, Copenhagen (DK) 2007, 3XN Architects

White-Wood
Main Phase

Black-White-Grey
Main Phase

117|1 **Trend monitoring** uses 'filtered' image data to visualise significant design elements and colour profiles.

Living Ergonomics – Movement Concepts for the Architecture of Work Environments

Text Burkhard Remmers

The term ergonomics *is an artificial word composed of the Greek words 'ergon' (work) and 'nomosnomos' (law, principle). Ergonomics is the scientific study of human work and deals with the optimal adaptation of work to the characteristics and capabilities of human beings.*

cf: http://www.dguv.de/ifa/de/fac/ergonomie/index.jsp (accessed on 18.11.2011)

Despite advances in occupational healthcare, increasingly clever ergonomics, and a reduction in exposure to physical strain, medical costs are exploding and the number of sickness absences is rising. It seems paradoxical that in recent years the very place in which physiological strains have been reduced to a minimum – the office – is where musculoskeletal disorders have been increasing significantly. Doesn't this indicate that it's high time to examine and rethink the approach to ergonomics employed so far? What does this imply for product design, or for the appreciation of human beings? And last but not least, for models of organisation and office buildings? With the development of a new sitting concept as example, this contribution illustrates backgrounds and interactions and identifies the perspectives of positive, human-oriented ergonomics. The shifting paradigm of ergonomics from reduction, statics, and a one-dimensional conception of efficiency towards enrichment, dynamics, and holistic well-being means that we also need to think of architecture in a new way: as a living environment in which the biological requirements of the human organism are met.

Core competence of dynamic sitting

Wilkhahn is an international specialist for development, manufacture, and marketing of high-quality furniture for office, conference, and communication spaces. The company has been working on movement concepts for office work for the past four decades. Back in 1972 it asked product designer Prof. Hans Roericht to conduct an extensive study titled 'From Inflexible to Dynamic Seating'. The results of this study led to the development of a one-legged standing aid by design studio ProduktEntwicklung Roericht (PER) and to the development of a swivel chair by Wilkhahn in 1980, which has established 'dynamic' sitting as a characteristic of healthy office chairs all over the world. After developing several chairs with numerous innovative details, the company initiated a new project in 2005. The idea behind it was to contribute a further fundamental development to achieve a leap in innovation similar to the one 25 years earlier.

The development plan included a one-year phase for fundamental studies and research, the results of which were to form the basis of the actual concept development. The procedure is based on the notion of a 'reset' to permit a completely unbiased investigation of different innovation potentials. In the first year various fields of inquiry were studied that influence office work in its entirety.

Project room and methodology

In order to give the project appropriate significance within the company, the managing partner assumed leadership of the project. A dedicated space was provided to allow undisturbed and unhindered work on the project beyond everyday business. The walls and tables of the room served as a 360 degree display of the information and results obtained from the research fields. Synchronous visualisation ensured constant presence of all information and made cross-links, inconsistencies, and dependencies immediately apparent. Regarding the topics of material and technologies, samples were collected from various areas such as sports shoes, swim fins, or toothbrushes, the geometries and structures of which were suitable for fulfilment of multiple functions, such as partial capacity for movement. At the same time, everything customary in an office chair was reconsidered and questioned: from rollers, arm rests, shell or frame constructions, to completely new 'standing' seating ideas. All these ideas were built, tested, and assessed, either as functional components, model structures, or useable prototypes (120|1 and 120|2).

New connections

A test arrangement for visual perception of comfort proved to be particularly helpful. When is a chair visually perceived as inviting or comfortable? For this purpose, the developers fixed the seats and backs of four office chairs at different angles, including an upright backrest with a seating area inclined downwards ('attention' position), various opening angles and tilt positions, and an obviously comfortable and very large

119|1 The applicable standard in dynamic sitting to this day: the designer Werner Sauer on the **office chair classic** FS-Line 1980 and 2005

Research fields:

- *General social developments in international economies, such as long-term trends in the primary, secondary, and tertiary sector; changes in social value systems with regard to concepts of work; physiological developments regarding body height and weight*
- *Dynamic changes within the world of office work, which are mainly caused by information and communication technology and lead to new forms of office work and organisation models worldwide*
- *Most recent findings on health, psychology, and ergonomics*
- *Screening for new technologies and so-called intelligent materials in all sectors*
- *Comprehensive value analysis of relevant office chairs including analysis of different kinematics models and seating characteristics*
- *Worldwide developments in ecological requirements*

opening angle ('lounging' position). The result of surveying 23 participants was surprising: assessment of 'appropriate' comfort is obviously influenced by social conventions, preliminary knowledge of ergonomics regarding supposedly correct sitting, as well as subjective perception. The combination of psychological, cognitive, social, and ergonomic aspects of well-being led to examination of a highly interesting field: new studies in health research. The developers analysed long-term studies by the Bertelsmann Foundation and studies by the ZfG (Centre for Health) at the German Sport University Cologne. The results indicate that the real cause of the rampant 'backache epidemic' and almost all other civilisation-related diseases lies in the way backaches are treated: therapies based on medication, rest, and passive treatment actually prolong the problems, because they switch off the body's own regulation systems, instead of activating them.

Pathogenic relief from strain

What do these findings imply for office work, work processes, and sitting? Wilkhahn contacted the ZfG and its head Prof. Ingo Froböse, who is a recognised expert in preventive and rehabilitation medicine, as well as a committed advocate of a new understanding of health. He explained the apparent paradox that a reduction in strain can cause a deterioration in health: especially in office work, the ergonomic strategies exclusively designed to reduce physical strain do not lead to a better state of health, but to a significantly worse one. The protection from excessive one-sided physical strain resulted in a permanent under-utilisation, while work is becoming significantly more demanding mentally. The combination results in a vicious cycle: lack of movement and stimulation lead to painful degenerations, which also give rise to psychological strain. In turn, the increased psychological pressure disturbs metabolic functions, thereby increasing physical complaints. The body is challenged less and less both on the way to work and within office buildings. Short distances, elevators, and the disappearance of tasks such as personally delivering files or archive materials as a result of using computers have reduced the physical activity required for completion of work to a movement of the fingers for operating a keyboard and a mouse. Studies have shown that the physical activity of adult men in Germany amounts to only 25 minutes a day on average, compared to the ten to twelve hours intended by the biological design of the body. Froböse also dismisses the common conceptions of ergonomically 'correct' or 'incorrect' sitting postures. Sitting still in an upright position as a sign of concentrated work leads to tension, tiredness, and headache over a longer period of time. Thus, these studies indicate that the 'corset philosophy' in the ergonomics of seating has led to a dead end: the claim of achieving maximum relief from strain on the body through complicated settings negates any incen-

120|1 **Models made of foam** at 1:1 scale can be produced and modified relatively quickly. They enable evaluating the proportions of complex, three-dimensional structures.

120|2 About 80 **hand-crafted model parts and complete models** were produced in the design process to reach the final result.

tive to move, thereby increasing the problem, instead of solving it. Scientific proof was finally obtained for what had been the basis of office chair development at Wilkhahn for almost four decades: the consistent promotion of movement for an active and dynamic sitting style.

Findings from biology

But what actually are healthy movements? As far as space for movement and body posture are concerned, all joint functions and positions that the body can carry out without pain are correct and important. Therefore, the new sitting concept should encourage movement that is natural and diverse, but also promote frequent changes between different sitting positions, in order to activate metabolic receptors. To reduce the risk of erroneous developments, the ZfG was asked in 2007 to find out to which extent the three-dimensionally mobile standing aid that was redesigned in 1992 actually promotes health. For this purpose, the office workplace of the test individuals was supplemented with the standing aid for a period of eight weeks. Participants were asked to document their use of the aid, and they were examined before and after the study. The results of the comparison surpassed expectations: utilisation of the standing aid not only employs and activates far more stabilising muscle groups, but also improves the coordination of the participants, such as for maintaining balance. This confirmed the central idea of our new sitting concept – the integration of natural three-dimensional mobility and muscle stimulation.

Learning from analogy to nature

The previous two-dimensional sitting dynamics reflect bending and stretching of the torso. If human beings moved analogous to this kinematic circumstance, locomotion would be restricted to sack-race-like movements. Therefore, the obvious choice was an alternative concept based on the natural joint functions of the body as a model. The movement of the hip as a centre of vitality and of the body became the decisive approach of the new concept. From the hip, the elasticity of the spine, the shoulder joints and the back, nape, and neck musculature, as well as the knee joints and the leg musculature can be stimulated as a comprehensive system. This is not limited to forward, backward, or lateral movements, but also includes a free combination of these in the form of rotation. Accordingly, the newly developed trimension allows completely natural three-dimensional motion sequences of seat and back, which follow all the directions of movement including rotation. The pivots correspond to the positions and functions of the human knee and hip joints. The centre of gravity of the body remains in balance in every position, and the supporting spring force increases synchronously with each

121|1 **Finite Element Analysis** for the right swivel arm, which takes up the knee joint function at the front and the hip joint function at the back: the load peaks are visible in the digital simulation.

121|2 The 'sitting comfort' component of the study: thin calibrated seating mats are used to measure **pressure distribution and pressure peaks** in the seat area and backrest. The new sitting concept also receives top scores in a comparative study.

movement. Supported rotational movements of hip and torso activate the entire locomotor system via specific muscle groups, especially the ones responsible for the deep musculature of the back, which are so important for stabilisation of the spine. This means that a significantly improved sense of well-being and ability to concentrate can be expected, compared to sitting on conventional office chairs. The typical backache associated with passive sitting should no longer occur. As simple as the concept may appear to be: it took another four years to represent the complexity of the natural dynamics of the body in terms of kinematics, and at the same time, fulfil the design objectives and cost targets set for the new office chair.

Design quality as a new dimension of ergonomics

Thus far, aesthetic quality as a direct influencing factor on well-being and performance has been a neglected aspect of ergonomics. The stress caused by sensory overload or over-pronounced features in the design change the biochemical quality of metabolic processes and, in negative cases, lead to physical discomfort, tension, and backache. For office chairs, this means that 'sitting machines' reminiscent of medical devices and skeletal constructions prevent a positive, intuitive, and natural access to the body's own competencies. Therefore, first-class design quality is far more than just 'nice to have'. As far as the psychological disposition is concerned, the same applies to physiological aspects: well-being is produced on an activating and stimulating level between stimulus reduction and stimulus overload. Since this level is defined by the overall spatial concept, the new office chair programme was designed with the aim of making the new sitting system evident, but unobtrusive enough to allow larger numbers of the chair to be integrated within different design concepts.

Evaluation and validation

Before series production, the ZfG conducted an initial scientific study with the new office chair in 2009. The interactions between body and chair in the case of 19 participants were investigated by using state-of-the-art measurement techniques. Study fields included a comfort and movement analysis, biological diagnostics, and a subjective documentation of individual perception, in order to examine if and how the new opportunities for movement were used and assessed. The study demonstrated that the development goals were, in fact, attained: the mobility of the chair corresponds to the physiological joint functions, and the users found the natural diversity of motion to be extremely comfortable and pleasant.

122|1 Result of the five-year research and development process: the first office chair in the world with three-dimensional, synchronously supported kinematics for maximum **natural dynamic sitting**.

After a development period of five years and an investment of EUR 3.5 million, the new programme was introduced to the market in late 2009 (122|1). The commercial success of the programme clearly shows that an investment in fundamental innovations and actively cooperating with research institutions pays off. The health factors, user expectations, and user acceptance were determined in collaboration with the ZfG. The fact that the programme was awarded top design prizes worldwide shows that health and aesthetics are not necessarily contradictory issues. These research results indicate that aesthetics are, in fact, a component of well-being.

Spin-offs for architecture

Human beings can't be calculated mathematically. They are individual and dynamic organisms, and their requirements change throughout the course of a day. Therefore, regarding the user as a subject rather than an object involves numerous implications that go far beyond the microcosm of an office chair. To this point, spatial programmes, functional allocations, and layouts in many building types are designed analogous to classical ergonomics, i.e. based on reduction, concentration, and short distances. Anything that doesn't appear to be directly productive is reduced to a minimum or eliminated completely. Are elevators really an improvement? Should central stairs become more important in regard to health (as well as organisational and social) aspects? Does the automated control of light and indoor climate do justice to human beings as dynamic systems? What kind of spatial organisation is required to activate human beings in physiological terms?

Health, considered against the background of demographic change and the increasing added value in office processes, is becoming a societal mega-subject. The scientific findings on the biology of human beings and their interaction with psychological and social factors offer a basis for planning and argumentation to also rethink the architecture of the working world: architecture as a space for movement, as a stimulating and activating structure, as a platform for social exchange and knowledge management, as well as an environment with aesthetic quality (116|1, 123|1 and 123|2). In short: architecture for the well-being of humans.

123|1 and 123|2 **Architecture as a space for movement**: the flowing spaces and open teaching islands grouped around the central staircase in Ørestad College in Copenhagen promote the development of social competence and vital body functions, thereby also advancing capacity for concentration and learning success. 3XN Architects, 2007

For further aspects of social and societal change cf. Back to Being Social » *p. 60, 69, Sustainable Urban Development* » *p. 71f., Trend Predictions* » *p. 102, Research Initiative 'Future Building'* » *p. 137*

Building Processes of Tomorrow – Trends, Scenarios, Development Axes

Text Alexander Rieck

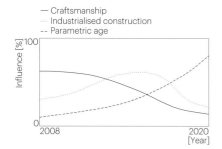

— Craftsmanship
···· Industrialised construction
-- Parametric age

124|1 Overview of the changing influence of **FUCON scenarios for the future**

1

FUCON project team at the Fraunhofer IAO: Alexander Rieck, Daniel Krause, Steffen Braun

2

Züblin, Thyssen Krupp, KOP, Schüco, LAVA, Drees & Sommer, Conclude, Design to Production, Würth, Brodbeck, OFB, IWTI, Steelcase, Saint-Gobain

The building industry holds a key position in the discussion on increasing demand for resources. While innovations have been promoted in other branches in recent years, e.g. in the automotive or shipbuilding industry, progress in the building industry has been very slow. However, in order to be able to meet the growing demands placed on buildings and cities, and to make the best possible use of the resulting opportunities, it is essential for businesses in the building sector to consider important future-relevant issues in advance. With this in mind, an innovation network, FUCON (FUture CONstruction), has been set up by the Fraunhofer IAO (Institute of Work Management and Organisation) in Stuttgart[1] in collaboration with companies in the building sector. The aim of the project is to establish trends and scenarios for future building and employ these to deduce the necessary consequences in the form of action strategies for companies and the sector. The developed scenarios are not only intended as visions, orientation, and guiding image for the construction industry, but also serve to encourage and support a constructive dialogue between all participants in the building sector. FUCON was created as a joint project, since a cooperation of complementary partners[2] was considered most suitable for advancing the necessary innovation process across all relevant branches, thereby sustainably strengthening the future market position of the companies involved.

How can the potentials of innovative information and communication technologies be used efficiently? How should the building process be organised to fulfil more complex tasks? How can the partners influence these events and how can they best prepare themselves for the future?

What does the architecture of tomorrow look like? How will cities be planned in the future, how will houses be built, existing buildings be renovated or demolished? These fundamental questions addressed to the building industry are aimed at a sector characterised by rigid structures and with internal processes controlled by laws and rules. Moreover, this system of regulation promotes a division of processes and accounts for the fact that those involved in building do not always consider the finished product, but instead merely focus on their own contractual scope. This can prevent innovation, even when certain technologies, such as digital fabrication or integrated data modelling, have long since become a reality in other sectors and could easily be adopted by the building industry.

The growing demands for more sustainability offer the building industry enormous chances, while simultaneously providing it with new impulses based on the introduction of innovative methods and technologies in planning and construction. All this leads to an increasing degree of change in all areas of the value creation chain of construction, as well as a change in processes and buildings – from initial design to demolition. Front loading, lean management, integrated planning with 5D building data models, public private partnerships (PPP), on-site RFID, and 'green' building with sustainability certificates are only a small selection of future-relevant topics that have impacted the building industry, building research, and policy in recent years.

Creation of scenarios

FUCON scenarios describe conceivable alternative developments in the building sector up to the year 2020 in German-speaking countries. For this purpose, significant processual, technological, structural, organisational, political, social, and global economy-related influences on the building industry were recorded. Based on this, scenario field analysis defines the subject focus of the scenarios and offers a selection of significant topics that play a central role in the further scenario process. This permits determining the important influencing factors that characterise future building. These key factors comprise the scope of topics relevant to future construction. The different scenarios are obtained by linkage of possible future developments of these factors through logical associations.

Scenario development involved conducting the 'Scenario Study FUCON – Ideals and Expectations for Building in the Year 2020' in 2008, in which statements by altogether 410 building-related experts from German-speaking countries were analysed. These statements served to test the plausibility of the entire scenario process and to compare it with experiences from practice. This initially resulted in seven consistent individual scenarios with logical workflows in technical and process-oriented terms. These were then condensed into three global scenarios: Crafts-

For questions on energy and handling of resources cf. Parametric Design Systems » *p. 52, Sustainable Urban Development* » *p. 72, 77, Understanding Buildings as Systems* » *p. 82–93, Common Sense Instead of High Tech* » *p. 94, Collaboration of Industry and Research* » *p. 130, Research Initiative 'Future Building'* » *p. 136, 139ff.*

Key factors
- *Degree of automation of construction*
- *Simulation, virtual reality*
- *IT support of building process*
- *Planning and construction process*
- *Execution and logistics of construction*
- *Life cycle management*
- *Building materials, utilisation, standards*
- *Building services technology and automation*
- *Energy management, building biology*
- *Possibilities and concepts for real estate property utilisation*
- *Degree of standardisation, modularity of building objects*
- *Guidelines, regulations*
- *Cooperations with the building industry*
- *Environmental legislation, Europeanisation*
- *Architecture, design*
- *Costs, availability of resources*
- *Health and environmental orientation*
- *Quality requirements, building quality*
- *Attractiveness of real estate property as capital investment*
- *Acceptance of technology, innovation rate*

For parameters, methods and application examples of trend research cf. Sustainable Urban Development » *p. 75, Trend Predictions* » *p. 105, Collaboration of Industry and Research* » *p. 130*

manship 2020 – this scenario is based on craftsmanship-oriented building processes in renovations and modernisations and focuses on their positive characteristics; Industrialised Construction 2020 – this scenario makes use of synergies based on other industrialised sectors that will result in an increase in efficiency in the building industry in the coming years; Parametric Age 2020 – this scenario offers major potential and combines great flexibility in planning and construction with high efficiency. However, this requires a long-term restructuring of the sector. Generally, it is decisive that these scenarios are likely to occur simultaneously, while covering different areas of the market that may also shift in the long run.

Craftsmanship 2020

A craftsmanship network as an individual service from a single source   At present, Germany has a stock of approximately 18.8 million buildings (including approximately 17.7 million residential buildings). Only about 0.8 percent of these are currently upgraded for energy efficiency purposes per annum. The federal government's target rate is a minimum of 3 percent per annum, which corresponds to 500,000 buildings requiring renovation. Compared to new construction, renovations are more complex, because available information on the object is often incomplete, and typical damages related to ageing aren't always immediately apparent. On top of that, innovative technologies, such as ventilation systems with heat recovery or air-tight windows have to be adapted to the existing building physics. The new energy-saving technologies make 'proper' planning of buildings increasingly multi-faceted, and the number of participants in the planning and building process is on the rise. As result, renovation projects become hard to manage and to calculate for many clients. This is further exasperated by the division of services required and the related responsibilities. Therefore, it is hardly surprising that the renovation rate remains very low, even though, from a financial point of view, an energy efficient renovation is worthwhile in many cases, as well as being highly desirable with regard to ecological and political aspects.

New, automated production technologies are already available to medium-sized trades and businesses. Processes can be made significantly leaner by consistent use of planning data. Unfortunately, rigid structures and an excessively traditional orientation of firms often obstruct the necessary increase in productivity. Traditional interfaces between the different trades are often no longer appropriate for the new technologies required in building, and their efficient use is prevented for reasons of liability. These divisions in the building process prevent individual trades from viewing a project comprehensively. Instead, they tend to focus on their own responsibilities within the project. However, why

For further aspects of the interconnection of planning, building and production processes cf. Operationality of Data and Material » p. 9, Industrialisation versus Individualisation » p. 21, 25, Material, Information, Technology » p. 31, Parametric Design Systems » p. 43

should clients accept this, considering that comprehensive, project-oriented approaches are in use in other sectors?. Yet, new service-oriented associations and networks that offer renovations as coordinated comprehensive products are currently on the rise. By acting as a partner here, the supplier industry benefits from being able to promote rapid development of innovative products. Better networking and coordination of all participants increases future efficiency of the entire construction process. Such lean management approaches originate in the automotive industry, where all processes are optimised by value stream engineering. However, the fact remains that the experience and craftsmanship skills of those carrying out construction work is still the basis of a successful renovation project. If the transformation of the building trade is successful, it will be possible to effectively combine existing traditions and knowledge with new requirements.

For the potential of use changes and renovations cf. Back to Being Social » *p. 61f*, *Sustainable Urban Development* » *p. 73*, *Understanding Buildings as Systems* » *p. 84*, *Common Sense Instead of High Tech* » *p. 99*, *Research Initiative 'Future Building'* » *p. 137*

Industrialised Construction 2020

Cost efficiency and product diversity through modularisation and serial production   While craftsmanship skills are particularly important for individual renovations, the huge demand for new residential space worldwide can only be met sustainably if efficient processes can be guaranteed, in addition to high fabrication standards. Since differentiation through design will continue to play an increasingly important role in the future, new fabrication processes will simultaneously have to enable a high degree of individuality of buildings. Related approaches can be observed in various other branches. For example, consider the drop in the number of development cycles in the automotive industry without deterioration in product quality and design in recent decades. This is facilitated by consistent industrialisation of the processes involved. Industrial fabrication has been used in the building sector for quite some time, with large product quantities considerably reducing production costs. As early as the onset of classical modernism the promise of extensive industrial fabrication gave rise to high expectations, which were only partly fulfilled. At the same time, they received a very bad image, such as in the case of precast concrete high-rise slab housing. The popularity of prefabricated houses, often based on wood frame construction, shows that a different stance is possible. The scenario 'Industrialised Construction 2020' continues the course of development of industrial fabrication, extending it both to commercial buildings and to certain areas of renovation. In an effort to make more extensive use of its potentials, future developments focus on modularised and platform-based systems. However, these systems can only be used efficiently if they are taken into account in the earliest planning stages. Current planning software uses Building Information Modelling (BIM) to generate a uniform and consistent building data model that can integrate all rele-

Building Information Modelling (BIM) *describes the generation and management of building data during the lifecycle of a building. It includes geometry, spatial relationships, geographical information, quantities, and properties of building components.*

cf: Hauschild, Moritz; Karzel, Rüdiger: 'Digitale Prozesse.' [Digital Processes.] Munich 2010, p. 105

vant building and product information. As result, the production machinery can be controlled directly, without interrupting system continuity. This permits achieving a high degree of individualisation in the industrial fabrication of buildings by means of so-called zero series, as well as profiting from the advantages of series production, including resource and cost efficiency and high fabrication quality. These factors also play a major role in the creation of sustainable buildings. In an effort to optimise these, methods such as 'front loading' (involving product-specific planning very early in the process) result in a departure from the bid invitation models used so far. The planner is in contact with the building industry at an early stage and makes use of their expert knowledge during planning, which also permits market-oriented pricing. In order to achieve an overall optimisation of these procedures during the developmental process, companies will increasingly function as system providers rather than product suppliers.

Parametric Age 2020

Individualised building for superior customer and environmental requirements through diverse processes   The scenario of parametric building combines the individuality of the craftsmanship-oriented scenario with the high efficiency and quality of the industrial scenario. Based on the possibilities that continuous digital fabrication processes offer, very complex building systems with a high degree of individuality and high site quality can be created in the future. In contrast to conventional planning, which involves purely geometric processes, parametric planning allows utilisation and mathematical combination of different parameters. The basic model remains highly flexible and changes automatically when a parameter is modified.

What seems very artificial and theoretical at first is, in fact, a fundamental principle of nature. Take, for instance, the definition of the human blueprint based on genetics. Rather than being a description of a finished 3D model of a human being, the interdependence of different cells is specified. As a result, we are all extremely individual, but have specific features in common, such as a nose in the middle of our face, with one ear on each side. The interesting thing about this biological system is the adaptability to environmental conditions across many generations. These planning generations can be simulated in the digital world, which means that parametrically planned building systems can be optimised through various stages of iteration before a specific status is 'frozen' for realisation.

In the future, the selection of the parameters and their prioritisation will be decisive. Numerous architects are currently experimenting with purely form-oriented design. This involves specification of a number of variables within a basic geometric structure, with shapes changing ana-

For the scope of individualisation trends cf. Operationality of Data and Material » p. 15, Industrialisation versus Individualisation » p. 24, Parametric Design Systems » p. 43, 52

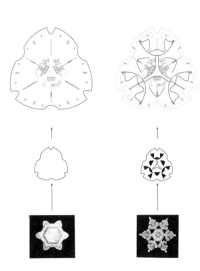

128|1 Study for floor plan development based on the **shape of snow crystals**. Snowflake Tower, LAVA

logously to the variance during replication. In the next step, physical properties are allocated to these geometries, and thereby optimised for an individual case.

The decisive step comprises the association of the shape with material and production properties. This allows the planner to create very efficient and individual buildings. The greater the complexity of individual building components, the greater the necessity of using parametric planning systems. Moreover, labs in academia and the industry are currently creating completely new materials. Innovative composite materials make it possible to build enormously tall buildings by offering a combination of reduced weight and great stability. For example, the extension of the 'Clock Tower' in Mecca – with 650 metres currently the world's second tallest building – was realised using a steel construction with a carbon fibre envelope. Materials with nano-optimised surfaces remove pollutants from the air and dissolve molecules hazardous to health. Technological innovations include weather-proof surfaces, self-repairing systems, active materials that can adapt to different climatic conditions, highly efficient insulation materials, or recyclable building components (cradle to cradle). As a model, nature is not exclusively focussed on efficiency, but is more interested in an effective multiplication of a system. Correspondingly, parametric planning systems will not create a fully automated planning process, but expand the conscious scope of the planner. This type of architecture can consequently be more bionic in nature than technically possible today. Whether this will lead to more nature-oriented buildings remains with the architect.

At this point in time, we already possess the knowledge to sustainably build and restructure buildings and cities. Moreover, thanks to a strong culture of innovation, Germany comprises a globally leading innovative and productive industry. Therefore, the necessary revolution of building construction is not hindered by a lack of technologies, but rather by the traditional structures of the building industry. However, nothing can stop these changes from occurring. More and more university graduates familiar with parametric processes are joining the professional world with the expectation that the building industry can realise the architecture they create.

'Cradle-to-cradle' *production is the opposite of the 'cradle-to-grave' model, in which material streams often don't take resource conservation into account. Instead of reducing the linear material streams of current products and production methods, the cradle-to-cradle concept is based on a life cycle development in terms of nutrient cycles: gained values are retained for man and the environment.*

cf: http://epea-hamburg.org/index.php?id=69&L=4 (accessed on 18.11.2011)

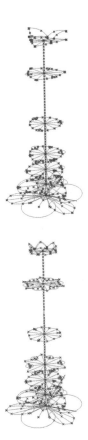

129|1 The entire shape of the building is modified by **changing individual parameters**. Study for the Snowflake Tower, LAVA

Motivation and Strategies for Collaboration between Industry and Research

Text Marcel Bilow

For parameters, methods and application examples of trend research cf. Sustainable Urban Development » p. 75, *Trend Predictions »* p. 105, *Building Processes of Tomorrow »* p. 125

For questions on energy and handling of resources cf. Parametric Design Systems » p. 52, *Sustainable Urban Development, »* p. 72, 77, *Understanding Buildings as Systems »* p. 82–93, *Common Sense Instead of High Tech »* p. 94, *Building Processes of Tomorrow »* p. 125, *Research Initiative 'Future Building' »* p. 136, 139ff.

Competition in the building industry, in particular among building product manufacturers, is fierce. The market demands products with a good price/performance ratio and enduring quality, that permit fast construction progress and, if the product is visible, have an attractive design. Knowledge on current trends and requirements is helpful in keeping product ranges up to date. But what are the trends that architecture and the building industry are currently subject to? What are the driving forces? What can new products offer?

Major areas certainly include energy conservation, sustainability (in a broad sense), and design requirements. Secondary aspects of these include transparency, adaptivity, free-form geometries, recycling, as well as surfaces and new materials. These trends are influenced by architects, who as designers are involved in the selection of products, as well as by legislation, which advances higher-order social objectives. Whereas before buildings were merely required to save energy, in the future they will be required to produce more energy than they consume – clear developments in this direction are discernible particularly with regard to building envelopes.

The reduction of CO_2 emissions and grey energy are related to energy conservation and also represent drivers of future developments. If a building no longer consumes any energy in the future, then the proportion of grey energy required for the manufacture of building products (or the amount partial to component materials) will become even more important. A catch phrase in this context is 'design for disassembly'.

These requirements put the entire building industry to the test, while simultaneously motivating it to think about new products. A rethinking process is taking place that encompasses design, planning, realisation, and subsequent operation of buildings. Manufacturers have to fulfil these demands and are consequently forced to optimise or redevelop their products and systems, in order to be able to prevail against the increasing competition.

The facade research group at the TU Delft has been working on this subject by carrying out two types of research: purely academic scientific research that aims to increase knowledge and advance scientific and social development, and practical applied research that forms a link to industry and manufacturers.

In its scientific research, the group develops market analyses, software tools, and planning strategies. Thus, trends and future requirements can be established by creating overviews of production and function and by research on the stages of development of individual topical aspects.

Practical applied research benefits from this scientific research. It collaborates closely with the industry to develop new products, adapt existing technologies, or test new materials for suitability.

A closer consideration of these processes from the perspective of a manufacturer allows their division into a variety of modes of work and motivations that pursue different aims:

- Optimisation
- Adaptation
- Expansion of application area
- Expansion of product range

Optimisation

One method of further development is the step-by-step optimisation of existing products. Window glass is a good example for illustrating how a product can be improved this way. Starting with single glazing with float glass, insulation glass was developed in response to increasing thermal protection requirements. The next step involved introducing noble gas in the cavity between panes. Sealing edges became more complicated to

Design for disassembly involves an evaluation of products on the basis of their recyclability and reusability as well as their production method and application within the building process. For example, a product composed of a large proportion of recyclable material should be fitted in a manner allowing simple disassembly and return to the material stream at the end of its lifecycle.

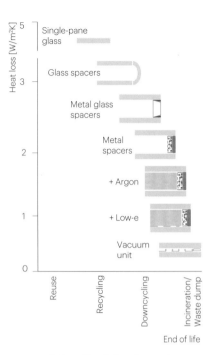

Heat loss [W/m²K]

Single-pane glass

Glass spacers

Metal glass spacers

Metal spacers

+ Argon

+ Low-e

Vacuum unit

Reuse — Recycling — Downcycling — Incineration/Waste dump

End of life

132|1 Evolution of insulation glass in relation to its recycling potential

Rapid Manufacturing (RM) *Term for generative processes that create preliminary stages of end products. The aim is to create a physical 3D part quickly, without manual detours, and based on CAD data. This involves reducing complex geometries to a large number of layered 2D production steps. Components or small series can be created with the successive layering procedures.*

cf. Hauschild, Moritz; Karzel, Rüdiger: 'Digitale Prozesse' [Digital Processes.] Munich 2010, p. 105

ensure long-term air tightness of insulation glazing. Research on sealants made it possible to meet these quality requirements over a usage period of about 20 years. Addition of selective layers such as hard or soft coating on the surface of the glass increases insulation even more or adds specific properties, such as sun protection. The further development towards triple glazing seems a logical consequence, but also gives rise to manufacturing problems due to increased weight. When pane sizes become very large, conventional facade and window systems are very difficult to use. Facade and window manufacturers are challenged by the need to adequately adapt the existing technologies.

The development of insulation glass is based on the necessity of improved thermal insulation qualities. However, a significant discrepancy becomes apparent when considering the recyclability of these elements (132|1). Simple float glass permits recycling, i.e. after melting it can be used again for making products of the same quality. Modern glass can only be downcycled, which means that the material can only be used to make products of inferior quality. The numerous coatings of the glass make proper separation and identification according to material type no longer possible; the panes are processed into container glass and turned into bottles and other glass products for everyday use. The recycling and reusability of window glass is certainly a motivation for research to develop a type of insulation glass that can be separated into its original components. Initial ideas on how simple separation of components can be achieved are already being discussed as potential research questions.

Adaptation

The industry is subject to constraints, due to increasing requirements specified by legislation, which necessitate constant adaptation of their product ranges and systems. In addition, development can also be provoked by design-related aspirations expressed by architects. The industry reacts by adapting existing systems to current trends and architectural specifications. While the manufacturing principles hardly change, the adaptation to new conditions is mainly manifested in the external appearance of the product.

Expansion of application area

If architects intend to maximise existing systems in terms of their dimensions, manufacturers may also be motivated to propose new developments. The student pavilion 'Black Box' of the TU Delft is a good example of this approach (133|1). The design of the cube-shaped pavilion – a small campus cafe with green facade – initially included an oversised door as a central entrance element. It soon became clear that folding glass wall systems supplied by the market leader were not available beyond an approved and tested maximum height of 2.30 metres. However, the company responded in a positive way: in cooperation with the university, an extra-large folding glass wall (4.50 metres in height) was developed on the basis of existing systems and including a number of necessary modifications. All required calculations and tests were carried out by the manufacturer at the factory, where they currently still serve to produce custom designs for other clients. Many companies follow the 'big is better' trend and can, for example, produce insulation panes 10 metres in height or width, as per request. This approach does not really involve typical research with the aim of developing new products; instead, it is focused on extending the existing limits of established systems and construction types. This requires integrated planning among all relevant disciplines.

133|1 **Folding glass wall** of the student pavilion 'Black Box', completed, TU Delft, 2007

Expansion of product range

If a company intends to develop a completely new product to extend the existing product range, formulating a concept is required, in addition to gaining knowledge on existing products offered by competitors in the intended field. In this regard, the research group at the TU Delft proved to be a good partner to the industry. A broad, as well as detailed body of knowledge resulting from years of education and research in specialised fields, including facade construction, glass construction, climate design, and comprehensive energy studies can be very useful. This is particularly the case when assessing the market and available products and technologies. In the course of several strategically planned research projects with various industrial partners, the research team developed a way to apply rapid manufacturing technologies to facade system construction, based on whether and to what extent technologies also referred to as 3D printing can support the production of facade components. The creation of an overview of available technologies, possibilities, and materials for processing was an important part of this research. This permitted limiting the project to the development of specialised components, which were then realised and tested as prototypes (133|2).

133|2 Detail of a **connector** made of laser-sintered stainless steel

An example of a particularly productive collaboration between the university and an industrial partner is the development of the facade design of the new Dutch headquarters of Solarlux in Nijverdal. This manufacturer of folding glass walls and slide-and-turn systems approached the facade research group with a plan to develop an innovative building with offices and a product warehouse. The project objectives included innovative use of in-house products in an extended area of application, as well as sustainable operation of the building. A rare, yet very positive feature of the innovative cooperation was that the partner was client, user, and facade manufacturer all in one.

A fully adaptive double facade

Double windows are nothing new. In the late 19th century, so-called 'winter windows' comprised an additional window fixed to the building exterior in front of the actual window during winter to improve insulation. The single window provided sufficient insulation in summer and prevented overheating of the window cavity. Fresh air could enter the building through open windows at night, and the building mass cooled off before the next day.

This principle was extended to the entire building envelope of the Solarlux Netherlands building. A primary thermally insulated wood-glass folding wall encloses the interior structure. A fully glazed, non-insulated slide-and-turn system is placed in front of it at a distance of approximately 100 centimetres. The double facade forms a buffer zone along three sides of the building. The resulting cantilever also offers sun protection when the sun is at its highest point in the sky. Those sides of the building that receive a high degree of thermal intake when the sun's position is low received an additional adjustable sun protection system. Both facade layers can be folded open completely. As result, various building envelope qualities can be achieved, depending on the weather conditions and the desired indoor temperature (134|1). The way the facade works is logical and self-explanatory; anyone can use it intuitively without requiring any background knowledge in technology or physics. User comfort is the primary objective.

The additional, completely openable exterior facade layer enables utilising solar gains or avoiding thermal overheating of the facade cavity (135|1). If the outside temperature drops below room temperature, the exterior layer is closed, solar radiation heats up the resulting facade cavity, and the interior facade can be opened as required. If the temperature in the cavity rises, the exterior facade can be opened completely, while the interior facade layer protects the inside of the building from wind and high outdoor temperatures. Between summer and winter seasons, the exterior facade can be opened in various ways so that the temperature of the facade cavity can always be kept at an optimum level. When closed, the exterior facade layer envelops a buffer zone with identical air pressure on all sides of the building. This makes it possible to open the windows without draught effects (135|2).

Studies show that individual productivity declines at the workplace, particularly when people are dissatisfied with the indoor climate and simply don't have the option of changing it. The double folding facade is intended to motivate users to interact with the building and actively assume responsibility of their individual work environment. This promotes communication with colleagues, as well as identification with the building and products of the company, which is also beneficial to productivity.

The client was particularly interested in the aspects of user comfort and

134|1 Transformability of the facade as seen from the exterior, Solarlux Netherlands, Nijverdal (NL) 2011, Wolfgang Herich (design), Van der Linde Architecten (execution)

Motivation and Strategies for Collaboration between Industry and Research

performance of the facade concept in operation. A long-term monitoring process is taking place in cooperation with the facade research group and Transsolar Energietechnik GmbH. It is designed to record performance data of the building in operation and allow optimisation of the building services engineering systems, in order to further reduce the primary energy demand of the building. The users are included in the evaluation throughout the measurement period by means of questionnaires. Initial problems specified by user critique have already been remediated within the building: screens on the interior of the facade now prevent glare along computer screens. Complaints about excessively dry indoor air in winter – building ventilation is exclusively natural – were met by increasing the number of planters and reducing ventilation.

While planning and design of the building are considered typical architectural tasks, evaluation and analysis of the building in operation comprise research activities. These support the company in becoming more familiar with the building (essentially designed as a self-test) and its functions, in optimising operation, and above all in determining new requirements relating to the products used and to adapt or develop these for additional projects.

The conclusion can be made that, from the view of both partners involved – the university on the one hand and the industry on the other – a future-oriented area of interaction can be recognised. This advances and generates knowledge for both academic scientific as well as practical applied research, which in turn gives rise to new input for both parties involved. The respective approaches, as much as they differ in detail, open up new horizons and lead to added value for all participants.

135|1 Variety of ways of opening the facade

a Cold winter day: both facade sections are fully closed, sun protection is not in use; thermal energy remains in the building, intermittent ventilation

b Spring/autumn: in case of appropriate solar intake, exterior facade remains closed for weather protection, interior layer is folded open completely; patio room-like work atmosphere

c Windless day with pleasant outside temperatures: both facade layers are open

d Hot summer day: interior layer is completely opened, interior layer is only opened for intermittent ventilation; building interior remains cool

135|2 View inside the **facade cavity**

Research Initiative 'Future Building' – Opportunities and Objectives

Text   Hans-Dieter Hegner

For questions on energy and handling of resources cf. » p. 139ff. as well as Parametric Design Systems » p. 52, Sustainable Urban Development » p. 72, 77, Understanding Buildings as Systems » p. 82–93, Common Sense Instead of High Tech » p. 94, Building Processes of Tomorrow » p. 125, Collaboration of Industry and Research » p. 130

The construction industry is not only the key to better infrastructure, improved living conditions, and more effective working environments. The building sector also offers major potentials for development with regard to sustainable economic operation and climate protection. The stock of existing buildings represents the largest consumer of energy in the economy (accounting for one third of total figures), and therefore also one of the areas responsible for the majority of CO_2 emissions. About 46 percent of CO_2 emissions caused by private households are attributable to heating and hot water generation systems. At this point in time, energy demands in Germany are chiefly covered by fossil fuels. Energy is as expensive as never before, but not because of an artificially produced shortage of resources, such as during the oil crises in the 1970s. Instead, this is attributable to steadily rising demands. In recent years, global economic developments have given rise to a disproportionate increase in the price of crude oil in the world market. The reaction to climate change and the associated improvement in energy efficiency represent a key area of the policies of the European Union and the German government. The targets set by the EU Council are ambitious: the aim is to decrease CO_2 emissions until 2020 by 20 percent as compared to 1990, and to increase the proportion of the primary energy consumption covered by renewable energies to 20 percent by 2020. The energy consumption predicted for 2020 is also to be reduced by 20 percent.

In addition to dramatically rising energy costs[1], enormous price increases have also been observed for important building materials, especially in recent years. From February 2005 to February 2008 the price of steel rose by more than 50 percent, while the prices of rebar steel and copper have doubled since 2000. The huge material flows in the building industry, which uses about 50 percent of all material resources and is responsible for approximately 60 percent of all waste, contribute to its important position in sustainable economic development. Therefore, economical and appropriate utilisation of material and promotion of recycling are essential components of building-related policies.

In addition to global issues, Germany also has some specifically local problems it needs to master. The subject of demographic change with a significantly ageing population has become a much discussed topic. While a decrease in the population from 82 million to about 70 million is predicted for the year 2050, the nature of population development in Germany is also essentially heterogeneous. Some regions register a significantly increasing population, while others are steadily becoming less populated. For example, the city of Eisenhüttenstadt near the Polish border had to cope with a 32 percent population decrease between 1990 and 2004. This development is connected to the demolition of disused urban structures and urban renewal. The trend towards increased ageing is virtually irreversible, while the immigration of foreigners only slightly dampens its effect. The proportion of people above 60 years of age will increase from its current figure of about 23 percent to 30 percent by 2020. In the future, the building industry needs to find answers to this problem, and others as well.

An increase in innovations in the building and real estate industry is imperative, if greater energy and resource efficiency is to be achieved, and to be able to react to demographic change. In the process, technical and organisational constraints will have to be overcome, with an emphasis on practice-oriented applied research rather than on basic research. Material and technology developments that often originate in areas other than the building industry need to be adapted for construction and integrated in its organisation. Examples of this include high-tech materials, vacuum products, or RFID-based processes, as well as products and systems for obtaining energy from renewable sources. The building industry requires stable framework conditions to adopt such technologies. These include technical regulations such as DIN standards, statutory requirements, or cooperations with companies.

1

Hegner, Hans-Dieter: 'Energieausweise für die Praxis. Handbuch für Energieberater, Planer und Immobilienwirtschaft.' [Energy Performance Certificates for Practical Use. Handbook for Energy Consultants, Planners and the Real Estate Industry.] Cologne/Stuttgart 2010

For further aspects of social and societal changes cf. Back to Being Social » *p. 60, 68, Sustainable Urban Development* » *p. 71f., Trend Predictions* » *p. 102, Living Ergonomics* » *p. 123*

For the potential of changes of use and renovations cf. Back to Being Social » *p. 61f., Sustainable Urban Development* » *p. 73, Understanding Buildings as Systems* » *p. 84, Common Sense Instead of High Tech* » *p. 99, Building Processes of Tomorrow* » *p. 127*

RFID (Radio Frequency Identity)
Identification and localisation by detection of emitted radio waves

Organisational implementation of the research initiative

The research initiative 'Future Building' of the BMVBS (Federal Ministry of Transport, Building and Urban Development) began in 2006. It aims to support small and medium-sized construction enterprises, to strengthen their competitiveness within the European market, and become market leaders in important sectors. The goal is to enable both the German government and the industry to react more effectively to social needs. The initiative is comprised of two basic pillars: grant-based research characterised by the commercial interests of the sector, and the building ministry's departmental research characterised by social and building policies.

The BMVBS has commissioned the BBSR (Federal Institute for Research on Building, Urban Affairs and Spatial Development) within the BBR (Federal Office for Building and Regional Planning) to conduct the research programme. While the BMVBS manages policy and organisation-related aspects of the research initiative, as well as assuming direct leadership of focus projects, the BBSR is in charge of project management and acts as contractual partner for the researchers.

The departmental research list is established by the BMVBS on the basis of political projects. The BBSR calls for bids on the topics, evaluates the offers in coordination with the BMVBS, and offers contracts for services. In the case of grant-based research, the BMVBS publishes the suggested research clusters in a public notice. These are directly correlated with the aims of the federal government during the ongoing legislative period and are jointly agreed on with the building sector within congresses on building research. The aim of these is to react to general social requirements, as well as to strengthen the market positions of primarily small and medium-sized construction and building material companies. Therefore, research is mainly carried out on subjects that promise maximum innovation content and the highest possible benefit for the sector.

One third of governmental financial support of the research initiative is allocated to departmental research and two thirds to grant-based research. Between 2006 and 2010, departmental research financed 175 research projects with a total volume of EUR 15 million. Support of grant-based research involves closing existing funding gaps with government funds. This is based not only on the applicant having an appropriate idea, but also individual or third-party funds. Being a major beneficiary, the building sector is intended to participate significantly in research activities. Support guidelines specify a 50 percent sponsorship. However, in reality the average proportion of government funds is 60 percent and that of individual or third-party funds is 40 percent. Between 2006 and 2010 a total of EUR 27 million of government funds were used to finance 200 research projects with a total volume of approx. EUR 40 million (138|1).[2]

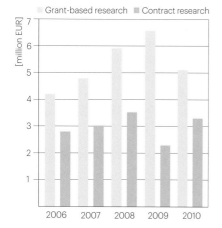

138|1 **Distribution of budget resources** for the Research Initiative 'Future Building'

2

Federal Ministry of Transport, Building and Urban Development (BMVBS) (ed.): Building the Future. The magazine of the Research Initiative 'Future Building'. Berlin 2010

The grant-based research funding tool can also be used for national co-financing of EU research projects in the field of building construction. The relevant guidelines of the BMVBS specify "that funding can be used as a contribution for national co-financing or projects with German participation for projects within the 7th EU Research Framework Programme, provided research activities are realised in the [...] specified fields."[3] However, this optional use of funding is currently underutilised. The federal government remains focused on the research initiative 'Future Building'. A continued increase of funds for building research is considered both desirable and effective, in particular relating to pilot and model projects aimed at energy efficiency and the application of renewable energies. Due to the newly created energy and climate fund, as well as the national climate protection initiative, funding for a pilot project for so-called energy plus houses ('Energy Efficiency House Plus') was initiated in 2011.

Departmental research

The first pillar of building research is contract research. It is organised as departmental research of the BMVBS and is entirely funded by tax money. The objective of this tool is to prepare and support government action. For this purpose, generating expert opinions and conducting studies on important legislative projects and political fields are assigned to, for instance, universities and research institutes. Examples of particular projects currently include:

- Update of the Energy Saving Regulation (EnEV 2012), further development of the Energy Performance Certificates
- Implementation of the EU Construction Products Directive (BauPVO) in Germany
- Further development of sustainable building (introduction of the German government's 'Sustainable Building Guideline', further development of the assessment system for sustainable buildings for additional building categories, Maintenance and further development of databases for building products such as Ökobau.dat or WECOBIS)
- Further development of code for building and modernisation with barrier-free or barrier-reduced access, implementation of DIN 18040
- Further development of guidelines for improving the building culture in Germany (competition and public procurement law, 'Art and Architecture Guideline' etc.)
- Adaptation of the government's technical construction code for federal construction projects (e.g. 'Fire Protection Guideline')

3

Announcement by the Federal Ministry of Transport, Building and Urban Development (BMVBS) of 19 May 2011 on awarding grants for research projects within the Research Initiative 'Future Building' in the year 2011, Federal Gazette, No. 84, 1 June 2011, p. 2013 [Bundesanzeiger Nr. 84, 1. Juni 2011, S. 2013]

For questions on energy and handling of resources cf. » *p. 136 as well as Parametric Design Systems* » *p. 52, Sustainable Urban Development* » *p. 72, 77, Understanding Buildings as Systems* » *p. 82–93, Common Sense Instead of High Tech* » *p. 94, Building Processes of Tomorrow* » *p. 125, Collaboration of Industry and Research* » *p. 130*

Current focus areas of departmental research:
- *Climate protection and energy efficiency*
- *Sustainability and building quality*
- *Regulations and building products*
- *Building culture and architecture and art*
- *Communication and broad application*

Grant-based research

Grant-based research is rooted in ideas that originate in 'the market'. Business and industry are invited to collaborate with academia and develop proposals for eliminating innovation deficits within the scope of specified focus areas. However, this means that the building sector itself also supports and funds the research projects and ensures a high standard of quality. All applications are subject to a competition procedure with preliminary examination by the BBSR and assessment by an independent group of experts at the BMVBS.

Particularly important results were achieved within the scope of the 'Energy Clusters'. The diverse efforts to achieve an improved integration of the most recent technologies in planning by technical specifications should be pointed out specifically. This relates to, for example, procedures on the energy evaluation of heat pumps or LED lighting in the Energy Saving Regulation (EnEV) and in DIN V 18 599. Testing technologies for utilisation of environmental energies is also an important field. For example, local heat recovery from domestic waste water is being studied at the RWTH Aachen. As far as the thermal activation of building components is concerned, significant progress in improving the acoustics of thermally active ceilings that don't permit application of suspended acoustic ceilings was made at the Fraunhofer Institute for Building Physics (IBP). A persistent focus is the utilisation of renewable energies in and on buildings. This involves meeting highest standards of technical efficiency, as well as achieving an architecturally appealing integration of technology in the building envelope or the structural complex. New types of thermally insulated, back-ventilated facades with thin-film PV modules have been developed within the scope of the initiative (141|1). Coloured solar panels have also become available in the meantime. Work on the integration of CIS photovoltaic elements with thermal insulation composite systems is currently in progress.

Current research clusters of application research:
- *Energy efficiency and renewable energies in the building area, calculation tools*
- *New concepts and prototypes for energy-saving building, concepts for zero-energy or energy plus houses*
- *New materials and technology*
- *Sustainable building, building quality*
- *Demographic change*
- *Regulations and contracting*
- *Modernisation of building stock*

Development of energy plus houses

The development and testing of energy plus houses comprises a special focus of the research initiative. The Technical University Darmstadt developed a house of this type in 2007 in order to take part in the Solar Decathlon Competition in Washington, D.C. Every two years since 2003 the U.S. Department of Energy has been holding this solar design competition, in which scientific institutions and universities from all across the world participate. Prototypes of the 20 best concepts compete during a 14-day contest at the National Mall in Washington, D.C. The most important target of the model houses, which are subject to performance tests in ten disciplines, is to produce more energy than consumed when fully occupied. In 2007 and 2009 the TU Darmstadt won first place in this competition.

Aim of the TU Darmstadt in 2007 was to build a house that not only consumes little and produces a lot of energy, but also to present an aesthetically pleasing architectural design.[4] A range of the most recent technologies was tested in and on the structure, including an innovative slat facade that provides shading and privacy from views, but also generates electricity via integrated photovoltaic elements. This was supplemented by highly insulating windows (partly with quadruple glazing) and vacuum insulation in the walls, floors, and ceilings. Innovative technical systems and energy-saving household devices complemented the project. Under optimal conditions, the solar cells can produce 12.5 kW of power. The two-story prototype with a living area of approximately 80 m² for the competition in 2009 combined high living comfort, energy-saving and -generating systems, and intuitive building control (143|2).[5] Minimising energy requirements was achieved by using highly insulating, air-tight building components for the thermal envelope in conjunction with ventilation system control and heat recovery. Air-conditioning is based on a reversible heat pump (heating and cooling) that withdraws energy from the surrounding air. In the case of a generally required controlled building ventilation system, technical building components such as radiators are no longer required. The heat pump permits simple energy transfer, and it can also be used in various climate conditions (from Mediterranean to cold). For good results in the climate of Washington, D.C. the house was equipped with additional cooling technology in the form of a controllable PCM cooling ceiling. The building envelope was optimised for energy generation and equipped with various PV technologies. Highly efficient, opaque, mono-crystalline PV cells were employed in the roof area, while thin-film cells were used on the facade.

The BMVBS used the 2007 house by the TU Darmstadt as a basis for their own presentation and exhibition pavilion, which displayed the concept in six metropolitan regions during a tour of Germany from 2009 to 2011 (142|1 and 142|2). The house found its final home in a development area called 'Phoenix See' in Dortmund in July 2011.

Combining property with mobility

The energy plus house of the TU Darmstadt was used to demonstrate the basic feasibility of combining intelligent building energy supply with environmentally friendly individual transportation. For this purpose, an electric vehicle that consumes 0.14 kWh/km was provided at an exhibition of the house in Essen in 2010. With an installed photovoltaic output of 19 kW, the building can supply nearly 14,000 kWh/a, which theoretically provides the vehicle with a range of up to 80,000 kilometres per annum. The two buildings by the TU Darmstadt illustrate that the current state of development of individual components is already highly advanced. An integration of both in an initial pilot project that encompasses living and

141|1 Thermally insulated, back-ventilated facade with **thin-film PV modules** on a building of the TU Dresden

4
Hegger, Manfred (ed.): 'Sonnige Zeiten.' [Sunny Times.] 'Solar Decathlon Haus Team Deutschland 2007.' [Solar Decathlon House Team Germany 2007.] Wuppertal 2008

5
Hegger, Manfred (ed.): 'Sonnige Aussichten.' [Sunny Prospects.] 'Das surPLUShome des Team Germany zum Solar Decathlon 2009.' [The surPLUShome of Team Germany for the Solar Decathlon 2009.] Wuppertal 2010

PCMs (Phase Changing Materials) *store thermal energy by triggering a phase change through the supply of thermal energy in a defined temperature range (normally from solid to liquid). Paraffins or salt hydrates are often used for this. PCMs can store significant amounts of thermal energy in a small space (storage vessel) or in building materials (such as through micro-encapsulation) to increase the thermal capacity that can be activated in spaces.*

cf: Voss, Karsten; Musall, Eike: 'Nullenergie-gebäude.' [Net Zero Energy Buildings] 'Internationale Projekte zum klimaneutralen Wohnen und Arbeiten.' [International Projects of Carbon Neutrality in Buildings] Munich 2011, p. 182

142|1 **energy plus house** as exhibition and presentation pavilion of the BMVBS

142|2 **Southern facade details**, exhibition and presentation pavilion of the BMVBS

6

http://www.bbr.bund.de/cln_015/nn
_22808/DE/WettbewerbeAusschrei-
bungen/PlanungsWettbewerbe/
AbgeschlWettbewerbe_table.html
(accessed on 05.09.2011)

Monitoring *is a systematic timeresolved capture, analysis, and evaluation of the operating data of a building using a data acquisition system, normally as part of the central building control system.*

cf. Voss, Karsten; Musall, Eike: 'Nullenergie-
gebäude.' [Net Zero Energy Buildings] 'Internationale Projekte zum klimaneutralen Wohnen und
Arbeiten' [International Projects of Carbon Neutrality in Buildings] Munich 2011, p. 182

mobility on a permanent and equal basis was desirable. Progress in the long overdue combination of architecture with new forms of mobility with regard to energy and functional aesthetics is to be achieved within further pilot buildings. The intention is also to create projects that act as a permanent 'showcase' for experts and the population, serving to demonstrate current state-of-the-art technology. The performance in operation of individual components requires testing by means of monitoring, which can also be used to gather experiences for broader application. This is also intended to promote a closer interdisciplinary collaboration of architecture, the automotive industry, energy supply, and building services engineering.

With this aim in mind, in summer 2010 the BMVBS held an interdisciplinary competition for creation of a energy plus house with electromobility,[6] which was intended as an open interdisciplinary design competition for higher education institutions in collaboration with planning offices. The goal was to show that an energy plus-standard building can supply itself and its residents, as well as several vehicles, with an average annual vehicle range of approximately 30,000 kilometres in the annual balance exclusively by use of environmental energy. In this regard, the electrical storage capacity incorporated in the house and the vehicles is of central importance. It serves as a buffer for the supply of the house and vehicles with electricity and can, in association with an intelligent network, provide storage functions. The research and pilot project was to be realised at an easily accessible location in the Fasanenstraße in Berlin City-West. The competition specified that the pilot building had to ostensibly meet the modern living requirements of a four-person household, clearly show its function as an energy supplier, and integrate a car port for electric vehicles (143|1).

The pilot project was also required to provide a clear answer to questions of sustainability. For example, aims included ensuring complete recyclability of the house, but also allowing conversion to different uses and flexibility, while maintaining very high living comfort. A complete assessment of sustainability is conducted in the course of the design process and erection of the building. In the meantime, the BMVBS concluded a design contract with the winning team, made up of the University of Stuttgart, ILEK (Institute for Lightweight Structures and Conceptual Design) and the Werner Sobek group of companies. Construction of the building was scheduled to be completed by the end of November 2011, followed by a scientifically supervised 3-month trial period of the project. In early 2012 a test family moved in and research studies are ongoing.

The completed project comprises a residential house for a four-person household with approximately 130 m² on two floors.[7] A so-called showcase for parking the vehicles and for accommodation of the charging infrastructure required for electromobility is located in front of the house. In order to reflect the mobility requirements of a family, vehicles included an electric primary family car, an electric secondary family car, and an electric two-wheeler (pedelec or electric scooter). The so-called energy core of the house is located between the two-story living area and the showcase in front and accommodates all the technical systems of the building and supply-intensive sanitary rooms. The house is equipped for a three-year monitoring, in order to gain information on future developments through a series of scientific tests.

In addition to the BMVBS, there is an increasing number of private project developers who support the creation and further development of energy plus houses within their own projects. In this regard, the link between real estate and mobility advanced by the BMVBS is an important driver, and the BMVBS intends to promote and follow related developments. For this purpose, the research initiative 'Future Building' will serve to provide opportunities to gain support for further pilot projects. The aim is to develop similarly innovative buildings all across the country and to assess these in joint research and development networks, both in the building and automotive sector.

7

http://www.bmvbs.de/SharedDocs/DE/Artikel/B/neues-energie-plus-haus-berlin.html (accessed on 05.09.2011)

143|1 Project for a **energy plus house with electromobility** in Berlin

143|2 **energy plus house** of the TU Darmstadt at the Solar Decathlon 2009 in Washington, D.C.

144–145|1 **Ørestad College**, Copenhagen (DK) 2007, 3XN Architects

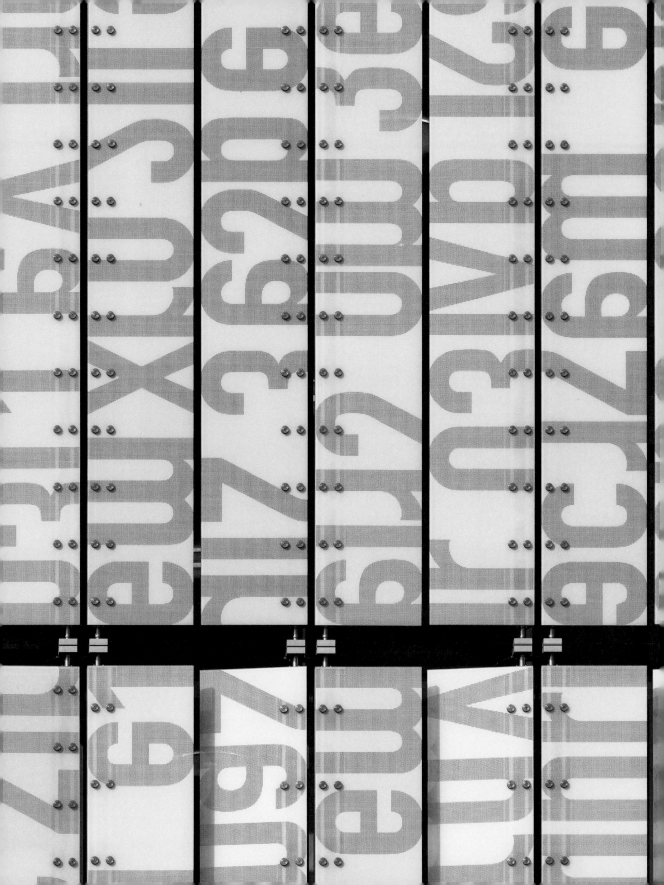

Partners

 BAU 2013

Sponsors and scientific partners

Bundesinstitut
für Bau-, Stadt- und
Raumforschung
im Bundesamt für Bauwesen
und Raumordnung

ETH Zurich:
Chair of Architecture and Digital Fabrication

ETH Zurich:
Chair of Computer-Aided Architectural Design

**Georg Simon Ohm University of
Applied Sciences**:
Professorship in Construction and Technology

**University of Applied Sciences
and Arts Hildesheim**:
Institute International Trendscouting

Technische Universität Braunschweig:
Institute for Building Services and Energy Design

Technische Universität Dortmund:
Department for Urban Design

Technische Universität Dresden:
Institute of Construction Informatics

Graz University of Technology:
Institute of Architecture Technology

Technische Universität München:
Faculty of Architecture

University of Stuttgart:
Institute for Lightweight Structures and
Conceptual Design

One idea revolutionises loft conversion

More than 65 years ago, Villum Kann Rasmussen from Denmark had the idea of introducing light, air, and quality of life into roof spaces. He wanted to transform dark, unused loft spaces and attics into open rooms flooded with light, and in 1942 he developed the first roof window – at that time just a simple wooden skylight. With Velux – a combination of "Ve-" for ventilation" and "Lux" for light – Rasmussen found a fitting name for his vision.

Ideas and innovations that set standards   Products characterised by compatibility and ranging from skylights for pitched and flat roofs and solar collectors to sun protection systems make it possible to achieve ideal lighting conditions through natural daylight and to improve living comfort as well. Intelligent additions to the product line, such as rain sensors and automatic heat protection ensure a natural, healthy, and comfortable indoor climate. The correct use of daylight and heat also improves a building's energy balance. With demonstration projects such as SOLTAG, Atika, and Model Home 2020 Velux intend to show how low-energy houses with good natural lighting conditions can be developed and conceived for the future.

Guaranteeing quality   The spirit of discovery displayed by its founder still shapes the company's activities today, with a diversity of new ideas and the development of innovative new approaches and products being actively encouraged. The aspects of energy balance, living quality, design, and functionality are all taken into consideration.

Before introducing them into the market, Velux subject their new developments to extensive testing in test laboratories and quality controls in field trials. For example, roof windows are subjected to extreme climatic conditions in the company's in-house laboratories. Rain loads and the forces that impact windows during storm conditions are simulated in wind tunnel experiments. These exhaustive testing procedures ensure that products meet highest quality standards.

Today, as the leading manufacturer of roof windows, the Velux group employs more than 10,000 employees in over 40 countries, including roughly 1000 in Germany alone.

VELUX Deutschland GmbH
Gazellenkamp 168
D–22527 Hamburg
T +49 (0)40 54 707 0
F +49 (0)40 54 707 707
E info@velux.com
www.velux.de

Image credits

Our sincere thanks to all those involved in the production of the book for letting us use their original images, granting permission for reproduction, and providing information. Photographs without credits either originate from the archives of the architects or the magazine 'DETAIL, Zeitschrift für Architektur + Baudetail'. Despite intensive efforts, it was not possible to determine the originators of some photographs and images. However, copyrights of the holders are retained. Related information is welcome.

Cover

Jasper James, London/Beijing

Operationality of Data and Material in the Digital Age

6|1–19|2 Gramazio & Kohler, ETH Zurich

Industrialisation versus Individualisation – New Methods and Technologies

22|1 Wolfgang Feierbach, Altenstadt
23|1 Therese Beyeler, Bern
25|1–27|1 Karlsruhe Institute of Technology - Building Lifecycle Management Section

Material, Information, Technology – Options for the Future

28|1–29|1 © zieta prozessdesign
31|1–32|2 Chair of CAAD, ETH Zurich
33|1 Tobias Madörin
34|1–37|1 © zieta prozessdesign
37|2 Chair of CAAD, ETH Zurich
38|1–38|2 © zieta prozessdesign
39|1 Fei Company, Courtesy Philippe Crassous
39|2 Tomlow, J.: Das Modell. Antoni Gaudís Hängemodell und seine Rekonstruktion. Neue Erkenntnisse zum Entwurf für die Kirche der Colònia Güell. Mitteilungen des Instituts für leichte Flächentragwerke (IL), Bd. 34. Stuttgart 1989
[The Model : Antoni Gaudí's Hanging Model and its Reconstruction - New Light on the Design of the Church of Colonia Güell – IL34, Communications of the Institute for Lightweight Structures (IL) University of Stuttgart, 1989]
40|1 © zieta prozessdesign
41|1 Chair of CAAD, ETH Zurich
41|2 Tobias Madörin

Parametric Design Systems – a Current Assessment from the Designer's Viewpoint

43|1 Werner Huthmacher, Berlin

44|1 Zaha Hadid Architects, London
45|1 Courtesy of Lacoste, Zaha Hadid Architects, London
45|2–45|4 Zaha Hadid Architects, London
45|5 Nils Fischer, London
46|1 Virgile Simon Bertrand, Hong Kong
46|2–49|3 Zaha Hadid Architects, London
50|1 Nils Fischer, London
51|1–52|1 Zaha Hadid Architects, London
53|1 Hufton + Crow Photography, London
55|1–56|1 Zaha Hadid Architects, London
57|1 Iwan Baan, Amsterdam

Return to Social Concerns – New Perspectives in Contemporary Architecture

59|1 Frank Kaltenbach, Munich
60|1–60|2 Iwan Baan, Amsterdam
61|1 Timothy Hursley, Little Rock/AR
61|2 Druot, Lacaton & Vassal, Paris
62|1 Iwan Baan, Amsterdam
62|2 atelier d'architecture autogérée, Paris
64–65|1 Iwan Baan, Amsterdam
66|1–66|2 Elemental/Tadeuz Jalocha, Santiago de Chile
67|1–68|2 Iwan Baan, Amsterdam
69|1 Christian Schittich, Munich
69|2 Brian Benson, London

Sustainable Urban Development in a Relational Framework

74|1 Chair for Spatial Development, TU Munich, Design: Anne Wiese
75|1 Chair for Spatial Development, TU Munich
76|1 Nemeth, Isabell: Methodenentwicklung zur Bestimmung von Potenzialen der Energieeffizienzsteigerung im Haushalts- und GHD-Sektor. [Development of methods for potential improvement in energy efficiency in the domestic and commerce, trade and service sectors.] Diss. TU Munich, 2011. Design: Anne Wiese
76|2 Chair for Spatial Development, TU Munich, Design: Anne Wiese
76|3 Nemeth, Isabell: Methodenentwicklung zur Bestimmung von Potenzialen der Energieeffizienzsteigerung im Haushalts- und GHD-Sektor. [Development of methods for potential improvement in energy efficiency in the domestic and commerce, trade and service sectors.] Diss. TU Munich, 2011.
77|1 Nemeth, Isabell: Methodenentwicklung zur Bestimmung von Potenzialen der Energieeffizienzsteigerung im Haushalts- und GHD-Sektor. [Development of methods for potential improvement in energy efficiency in the domestic and commerce, trade and service sectors.] Diss. TU Munich, 2011. Design: Anne Wiese

79|1 Nemeth, Isabell: Methodenentwicklung
zur Bestimmung von Potenzialen der Energieeffizienzsteigerung im Haushalts- und GHD-Sektor.
[Development of methods for potential improvement
in energy efficiency in the domestic and commerce,
trade and service sectors.] Diss. TU Munich, 2011.
79|2 Chair for Spatial Development, TU Munich
80|1 Clément Guillaume/Getty Images
81|1 Christian Richters/View/arturimages

**Understanding Buildings as Systems – Location
as Identity Generator**

84|1 Transsolar
84|2 Anja Thierfelder, Stuttgart
85|1 Transsolar
85|2 Adrià Goula, Barcelona
86|1 H. G. Esch, Hennef
86|2 Transsolar
87|1–87|2 Voss, Karsten; Musall, Eike:
Nullenergiegebäude. Internationale Projekte zum
klimaneutralen Wohnen und Arbeiten. [Net zero
energy buildings. International projects of carbon
neutrality in buildings.] Munich 2011
87|3 Foster + Partners, London
88|1–88|2 Iwan Baan, Amsterdam
89|1 Tom Arban, Toronto
90|1 Bryan Christie, New York
91|1 Paul Crosby, St. Paul/MN
92|1–92|2 Ateliers Jean Nouvel, Paris
93|1 Transsolar

Common Sense Instead of High Tech

94|1–95|1 Adam Mørk/Velux Deutschland,
Hamburg
95|2 Jakob Schoof, Munich
95|3 Adam Mørk/Velux Deutschland, Hamburg
96|1 Hegger, Manfred et al.: Ökobilanzierung. Velux
Model Home 2020. 'Licht-Aktiv Haus' Hamburg.
Öko-bilanzierung des Velux Model Home in Hamburg-
Wilhelmsburg. Abschlussbericht. [Ecological
Balance. Velux Model Home 2020. 'LightActive House'
Hamburg. Ecological Balance of the Velux Model
Home in Hamburg-Wilhelmsburg. Final Report.]
Darmstadt 2011
96|2 Velux Deutschland, Hamburg
97|1 Adam Mørk/Velux Deutschland, Hamburg
97|2–98|1 Active House Specification, 2011
99|1 Velux Deutschland, Hamburg

**Trend Predictions – Approaches, Methods,
Opportunities**

102|1 IIT HAWK, Hildesheim
103|1 IIT HAWK, Livia Baum, Sabrina Feder-
schmid, Hildesheim

104|1 IIT HAWK, Anne Lange, Hildesheim
106–107|1 IIT HAWK, Jutta Werner, Hildesheim
109|1–109|2 IIT HAWK, Hildesheim
110|1 IIT HAWK, Livia Baum, Hildesheim
110|2 IIT HAWK, Janine Kalberlah, Hildesheim
111|1 IIT HAWK, Livia Baum, Hildesheim
112|1 Meike Weber, Munich
114|1 IIT HAWK, Hildesheim
116|1 Adam Mørk, Copenhagen
117|1 IIT HAWK, Livia Baum, Hildesheim

**Living Ergonomics – Movement Concepts for
the Architecture of Work Environments**

118|1 Wilkhahn, Bad Münder
120|1–120|2 Designstudio wiege, Bad Münder
121|1 Zentrum für Gesundheit [Centre for Health],
Cologne
121|2–122|1 Wilkhahn, Bad Münder
123|1–123|2 3XN Architects, Copenhagen

**Building Processes of Tomorrow – Trends,
Scenarios, Development Axes**

124|1 Fraunhofer IAO, IAT University of Stuttgart
128|1–129|1 LAVA, Sydney/Stuttgart

**Motivation and Strategies for Collaboration
between Industry and Research**

132|1 cf: Bloemen, Matthijs: Design for Disassembly.
TU Delft 2011
133|1 Solarlux, Berlin
133|2 Strauss/Research Project of Hochschule Ost-
westfalen-Lippe – University of Applied Sciences/Alcoa
134|1–135|2 Solarlux, Berlin

**Research Initiative 'Future Building' –
Opportunities and Objectives**

138|1 Bundesministerium für Verkehr, Bau und Stadt-
entwicklung (BMVBS) [Federal Ministry of
Transport, Building and Urban Development], Berlin
141|1 Bernhard Weller, TU Dresden
142|1–142|2 Bundesministerium für Verkehr, Bau und
Stadtentwicklung (BMVBS) [Federal Ministry of
Transport, Building and Urban Development], Berlin
143|1 Bundesministerium für Verkehr, Bau und Stadt-
entwicklung (BMVBS) [Federal Ministry of
Transport, Building and Urban Development], Berlin/
Werner Sobek, Stuttgart
143|2 Thomas Ott, Mühltal
144|1 Adam Mørk, Copenhagen

Subject Index

Imprint

Concept:
Sandra Hofmeister

Editors:
Cornelia Hellstern (project manager), Sandra Leitte

Drawings:
Ralph Donhauser, Nicola Kollmann

Translation into English:
Antoinette Aichele-Platen, Munich (D)
Dr. Yasmin Gründing, Burglengenfeld (D)
Alistair Gray, Whitby (UK)

Proofreading:
Mark Kammerbauer, Dipl.-Ing., M. Sc., Munich (D)

Graphic design, typesetting/DTP & production:
Christoph Kienzle, ROSE PISTOLA GmbH

Reproduction:
ludwig:media, Zell am See

Printing and binding:
Aumüller Druck, Regensburg

Bibliographic information held by the Deutsche Nationalbibliothek. The Deutsche Nationalbibliothek lists this publication in the Deutsche Nationalbibliografie; detailed bibliographical information is available on the internet at http://dnb.d-nb.de.

This publication is based on the contents and contributions of the opening event of the launch of the interdisciplinary communication platform "Zukunftsforschung in der Architektur" at BAU 2011 in the Macro Architecture Forum of the department DETAIL transfer (overall concept Meike Weber, project manager Zorica Funk, editor and presenter Sandra Hofmeister).

DETAIL Institut für internationale Architektur-Dokumentation GmbH & Co. KG, Munich
www.detail.de • www.detailresearch.de

© 2012, first edition

ISBN 978-3-920034-74-4

Authors

Marcel Bilow

Training as mason, Architecture studies at the Lippe and Höxter University of Applied Sciences in Detmold Academic assistant, areas of Structural Design and Freehand Drawing (Architecture), Materials and Interior Structural Design (Interior Design)
2001 Founding of design office raum204 with Fabian Rabsch and Markus Zöllner
2004–2008 Project leader for research and development in the areas of Design and Structural Design at the Lippe and Höxter University of Applied Sciences in Detmold under Prof. Dr. Ulrich Knaack
Since 2006 Member of the facade research group at the Technical University in Delft, doctoral thesis on the subject "International Facades"
2008 Founding of facade planning office imagine envelope b.v. in The Hague with Ulrich Knaack and Tillmann Klein

Petra von Both

Studies in IT and Architecture at the universities of Koblenz, Kaiserslautern, and Karlsruhe
1997 Collaboration for Bilfinger Berger in the area of acquisitions and cost calculation
1998–2004 Research Assistant at the Institute for Industrial Building Production at the University of Karlsruhe
2004 Doctoral degree at the Institute for Industrial Building Production at the University of Karlsruhe
2005 Conducted research on Requirements Engineering and Process Modelling at the SCRI Research Centre, University of Salford
2005–2007 Collaboration with Nemetschek AG, Strategic Product Management
2008 Head of Corporate Strategic Development at Nemetschek AG, strategic advisor to the management board
Since 2008 Department of Industrial Building Production and Design (ifib) at the University of Karlsruhe Since 2009 Head of Faculty of Building Lifecycle Management at the Karlsruhe Institute of Technology
Since 2009 Advisor to the Federal Office for Building and Regional Planning (BBR) in the area of BIM and IT, Humboldt Forum project, Berlin
Numerous specialist publications

Philipp Dohmen

Studies in Architecture at the University of Applied Sciences in Cologne, postgraduate diploma in CAAD at the ETH Zurich
2002–2006 Freelance architect in Cologne
2006 Lecturer for Element-Based Building at the University of Applied Sciences in Düsseldorf
2006–2010 Research Assistant at the Department for CAAD, Department of Architecture, ETH Zurich
Since 2006 Consultant for parametric process design, process-design.net, Zurich
Since 2008 Head of Digital Tools department, Halter Unternehmungen, Zurich
Joint Director of the Institute for FiDU Technology with Oskar Zieta, ETH Zurich

Nils-Peter Fischer

Studies in Architecture at the Technical University of Darmstadt and at the Università Roma
Collaboration for ABB Architekten and Bernhard Franken Architekten in Frankfurt
Independent consultant for, among others, projects by Massimiliano Fuksas and participation in research projects by the European Space Agency
Since 2004 Assistant at Zaha Hadid Architects in London, since 2008 Associate
Founding, Head of the "Computational Design Research Group" (CODE) at Zaha Hadid Architects, a project-independent team developing internal tools and methods for form finding and rationalisation

Sabine Foraita

Studies in Industrial Design at the Hochschule für Bildende Künste (HBK) in Braunschweig
Professional activity for the industry
Postgraduate studies in Art and Design at the HBK Braunschweig
Lecturer at various universities
2005 Doctorate degree at the HBK Braunschweig
Since 2006 Department of Design Science and Design Theory at the University of Applied Science and Art (HAWK) in Hildesheim

Fabio Gramazio

Studies in Architecture at the ETH Zurich
1994–2000 Co-founder of the art project etoy
1996–2000 Research Assistant at the Department for Architecture and CAAD, ETH Zurich, under Prof. Gerhard Schmitt
2000 Founding of the architectural practice Gramazio & Kohler with Matthias Kohler
Since 2005 Assistant Professor of Architecture and Digital Fabrication at the Department of Architecture, ETH Zurich
Since 2010 Professor of Architecture and Digital Fabrication at the Department of Architecture, ETH Zurich